The End of Loser Liberalism

Making Markets Progressive

By Dean Baker

Published by the Center for Economic and Policy Research
Washington, DC

Published by the Center for Economic and Policy Research
1611 Connecticut Ave. NW, Suite 400
Washington, DC 20009
www.cepr.net

Cover photo by Helene Jorgensen

Cover design by Justin Lancaster

ISBN: 978-0-615-53363-6

Contents

Acknowledgments

I have benefitted enormously from discussing the ideas in this book with my colleagues at the Center for Economic and Policy Research, Eileen Appelbaum, Heather Boushey, Helene Jorgensen, David Rosnick, John Schmitt, and Mark Weisbrot. I also received helpful comments on the manuscript from Alan Barber, Kris Warner, and Nicole Woo. Jane Farrell helped with the graphs. Pat Watson did his usual outstanding job editing the book.

I thank Helene, Walnut, Olive, and Kiwi for tolerating my neglect while writing the book. And Biscuit deserves special note for allowing himself to be the poster boy of Loser Liberalism.

Chapter 1

Upward Redistribution of Income: It Didn't Just Happen

Money does not fall up. Yet the United States has experienced a massive upward redistribution of income over the last three decades, leaving the bulk of the workforce with little to show from the economic growth since 1980. This upward redistribution was not the result of the natural workings of the market. Rather, it was the result of deliberate policy, most of which had the support of the leadership of both the Republican and Democratic parties.

Unfortunately, the public and even experienced progressive political figures are not well informed about the key policies responsible for this upward redistribution, even though they are not exactly secrets. The policies are so well established as conventional economic policy that we tend to think of them as incontrovertibly virtuous things, but each has a dark side. An anti-inflation policy by the Federal Reserve Board, which relies on high interest rates, slows growth and throws people out of work. Major trade deals hurt manufacturing workers by putting them in direct competition with low-paid workers in the developing world. A high dollar makes U.S. goods uncompetitive in world markets.

Almost any economist would acknowledge these facts, but few economists have explored their implications and explained them to the general public. As a result, most of us have little understanding of the economic policies that have the largest impact on our jobs, our homes, and our lives. Instead, public debate and the most hotly contested legislation in Congress tend to be about issues that will have relatively little impact.

This lack of focus on crucial economic issues is a serious problem from the standpoint of advancing a progressive agenda. Mainstream economic conservatives already have an enormous advantage in national politics because they control most of the money that finances political campaigns. To add to that, they also use their money to buy directly into the national debate by funding organizations and projects intent on undermining important programs they don't like – as investment banker Peter Peterson has done with his decades-long crusade against Social Security and Medicare. But all the money in the world will hardly matter if progressives do not understand how basic, conventional economic policy militates against the interests of working people and the disadvantaged. If they don't even know what winning would look like, then the prospects for a progressive economic agenda are bleak.

For the most part, progressives accept the right's framing of economic debates. They accept the notions that the right is devoted to the unfettered workings of the market and, by contrast, that liberals and progressives are the ones who want the government to intervene to protect the interests of the poor and disadvantaged.

But this view is utterly wrong as a description of the economy and competing policy approaches. And it makes for horrible politics. It creates a scenario in which progressives are portrayed as wanting to tax the winners in society in order to reward the losers. The right gets to be portrayed as the champions of hard work and innovation, while progressives are seen as the champions of the slothful and incompetent. It should not be surprising who has been winning this game.

In reality, the vast majority of the right does not give a damn about free markets; it just wants to redistribute income upward. Progressives have been useful to the right in helping it to conceal this agenda. Progressives help to ratify the actions of conservatives by accusing them of allegiance to a free-market ideology instead of attacking them for pushing the agenda of the rich.

For the last three decades the right has been busily restructuring the economy in ways that ensure that income flows upward. The rules governing markets, written by the rich and powerful, ensure that this gravity-defying outcome prevails. The right then presents the imposition of rules that it likes as the natural result of unfettered market forces.

Rarely does this upward flow of income require a government check to the wealthy. But when the checks are necessary, they come. The Treasury and the Federal Reserve Board gave trillions of dollars in loans, at below-market interest rates, to the largest Wall Street banks at the peak of the financial crisis in 2008. These loans kept Goldman Sachs, Citigroup, and most of the other major Wall Street banks from collapsing, and the subsidies implied by the loans and guarantees to the world's largest banks were in the tens if not hundreds of billions of dollars. Yet somehow this massive intervention on behalf of these banks' executives, shareholders, and bondholders – some of the richest people in the country – is not viewed as interference with the market.[1]

While the bank bailouts were big news, there is no shortage of less-visible instances in which conservatives have long been eager for the government step in to support the interests of the wealthy. We'll quickly discuss seven examples here: continued support for too-big-to-fail banks, patent and copyright protection, restrictions on organized labor, corporate liability limitations, Federal Reserve monetary controls, trade and dollar policy, and housing policy.

Too-big-to-fail banks

To start with an easy one, how many "free market fundamentalists" have rallied behind efforts to break up "too-big-to-fail" banks? This one should be a no-brainer for any genuine believer in free markets. A too-big-to-fail bank is a

---

1 Supporters of the bailout have been eager to claim that the government made money on these loans. This is not honest accounting. The money was lent at rates far below the market rate at the time. No accountant would ever say that a below-market loan turned a profit because it was repaid. Providing a loan at below-market rates implies a government subsidy, and while Wall Street banks were able to get this subsidy from the government, millions of struggling small businesses across the country were not so lucky.

bank that everyone expects will be bailed out by the government if it gets in trouble, as happened in 2008. Because investors can assume that the government will back up the bank, they are willing to lend it money at a lower interest rate than if they thought the bank was standing on its own. How could any believer in the virtue of free markets support the existence of large financial institutions that borrow at a lower cost than their competitors because of an implicit guarantee from the government?

The fact that most of those claiming to be "free marketers" have overwhelmingly been on the side of the too-big-to-fail banks tells the world as clearly as possible that their motivations have nothing to do with a commitment to market fundamentalism and everything to do with a commitment to serving the interests of the rich and powerful. This is disguised as a commitment to the market for the obvious reason that doing things out of a commitment to free market principles sounds better than explicitly claiming to pursue policies that redistribute income from the vast majority of the population to the rich.

Patent and copyright protection

Patents and copyrights offer another example of how conservatives quietly support massive intervention by the government. Though we tend to think of them as integral parts of the free market, patents and copyrights are anything but.

Patents and copyrights are both explicit government policies to promote innovation and creative work. They reward inventors, musicians, writers and other creative workers with government-enforced monopolies for set periods of time, and these monopolies allow the holders to charge prices far above the free-market price. For example, the nation will spend close to $300 billion in 2011 on prescription drugs.[2] In the absence of government-enforced patent monopolies, the same drugs would cost around $30 billion, an amount that implies a transfer to the pharmaceutical industry of close to $270 billion a year, or about 1.8 percent of gross domestic product. It is close to 15 times current federal spending on the main government welfare program,

---

2 Center for Medicare and Medicaid Services (2011a), Table 11.

Temporary Assistance for Needy Families (TANF), and it dwarfs the money at stake from a main goal of progressives: eliminating the Bush tax cuts for the wealthy (**Figure 1-1**).

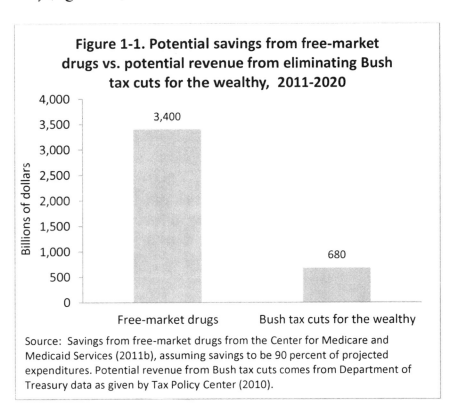

Figure 1-1. Potential savings from free-market drugs vs. potential revenue from eliminating Bush tax cuts for the wealthy, 2011-2020

Source: Savings from free-market drugs from the Center for Medicare and Medicaid Services (2011b), assuming savings to be 90 percent of projected expenditures. Potential revenue from Bush tax cuts comes from Department of Treasury data as given by Tax Policy Center (2010).

Copyright monopolies also involve massive transfers to companies like Microsoft, Apple, Time Warner, Disney, and Sony because the monopoly allows the companies to charge large sums for software, recorded music, and video material that would be available at no cost in a free market. Free-market fundamentalists should not be supporting this sort of interference in the market.

Restrictions on organized labor

Yet another area where the government intervenes in the market at the behest of the well-off to diminish the well-being of workers and the disadvantaged is labor-management policy. The accepted view is that progressives want the government to intervene to protect workers, while conservatives would rather let workers and management sort things out for themselves. That's not quite the story.

Though labor law provides protections to workers and their unions, it also constrains workers' power in important ways. For example, it is illegal to organize or honor a secondary boycott. If the workers at a restaurant go on strike and then arrange for the Teamsters to refuse to deliver food to honor the strike, the restaurant can enlist the government to deliver injunctions and impose fines against the Teamsters. If Teamsters officials ignore the injunction (e.g., they don't tell their members that they cannot refuse to deliver food to the restaurant), they can face imprisonment.[3] This is not the free market; this is the government intervening on behalf of employers.

Another example of how labor-management policy is rigged away from market forces is the fact that 22 states currently deny workers freedom of contract with their employers. Under "right-to-work" laws, workers are prohibited from signing contracts with employers that require workers covered by a union contract to pay their share of the union's costs. The law requires that everyone who is in a union bargaining unit – regardless of whether they are actually in the union – gets the same pay and benefits. The law also requires that the union represent workers in disputes with employers on issues covered by the contract, whether or not a worker is in the union. This means that if a worker who does not pay to support the union is fired, the law requires that the union represent the worker through any appeals process established under the contract.

While the law requires unions to provide the same benefits to all workers covered by a contract, right-to-work laws prohibit unions from signing agreements with employers that would require workers to pay for the benefits they are receiving. It in effect guarantees representation without taxation. This restriction of freedom of contract is not consistent with a free market. "Right-to-work" laws are just another way in which the right uses the

---

3 The Teamsters generally negotiate contracts that include a provision to the effect that they do not have to cross a picket line if they fear for their personal safety. There have been many incidents over the years in which truck drivers have feared for their safety upon seeing a union picket line.

power of the state to reduce the power and income of workers. Free marketers are perfectly willing to deny the freedom of contract to accomplish this end.

Corporate liability limitations

The modern limited liability corporation is another example of interference with a pure free market. Corporations do not exist in the natural world or in the free market; they have to be chartered by a government. They are artificial entities that can inflict damage on the public without the individuals at fault being held fully accountable. Limited liability means that the government allows corporations to harm individuals – for example, by allowing toxins to get into a community's drinking water – without the corporation's top management or shareholders being obligated to pay compensation. The victims (those drinking contaminated water in this case) are entitled to whatever assets are held by the corporation, but they cannot take the personal assets of the top managers or the shareholders.

By creating limited liability corporations the government is allowing the individuals who form a corporation to take the property (or even lives) of others without compensation. This is not a free market.

Federal Reserve monetary controls

A government policy with tremendous influence over economic outcomes is the power of the Federal Reserve Board in determining the level of employment. The Fed can foster growth and employment with low interest rates and expansionary monetary policy. But it can and often does deliberately raise the unemployment rate by raising interest rates. Moreover, the Fed's policy on holding assets like government bonds has an enormous impact on the government's debt burden, which in turn has redistributive implications.

Yet Fed policy receives little attention from progressives. We spend far more time arguing over jobs bills that will have a trivial impact on employment compared to the Fed's monetary policy. And we devote major lobbying efforts to tax or budget items that don't have a tenth of the impact on the debt as the Fed's decisions on its asset holdings.[4]

Figure 1-2 shows the lost output from the Great Recession, an event that could have been averted with competent Fed policy, compared with revenue that would be gained over the years 2011-2020 from eliminating the Bush tax cuts for the wealthy. As can be seen, the lost output from the Great Recession is more than five times as large.

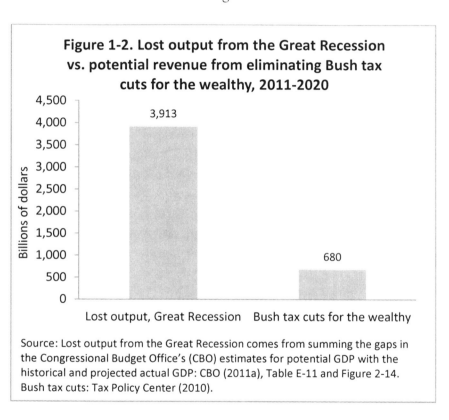

Figure 1-2. Lost output from the Great Recession vs. potential revenue from eliminating Bush tax cuts for the wealthy, 2011-2020

Source: Lost output from the Great Recession comes from summing the gaps in the Congressional Budget Office's (CBO) estimates for potential GDP with the historical and projected actual GDP: CBO (2011a), Table E-11 and Figure 2-14. Bush tax cuts: Tax Policy Center (2010).

---

4 The Fed currently holds close to $3 trillion in mortgage-backed securities and government bonds. As long as the Fed holds on to these bonds, the interest on these assets is refunded to the Treasury: in 2010 the refund was almost $80 billion. By continuing to hold these assets indefinitely, rather than selling them to the public (which would mean the Fed would no longer be able to refund the interest), the Fed would substantially reduce the government's interest burden in future years.

The right is happy to keep the Fed out of public debate since, as things stand, the right largely controls it. Conservatives promote an image of the Fed as an august institution, managed by high priests who are unsullied by the dirty back-and-forth of partisan politics. This view works out great for conservatives, since policy decisions by the Fed and for that matter other central banks typically have far more impact on the economy than most of the issues debated by Congress. The right manages to stir up big debates over relatively small matters, leaving it to control one of the most important levers of power in the economy. And this, the right would have us believe, is the work of the free market.

Trade and dollar policy

Another example of an area in which the right has almost completely controlled the debate, and therefore the policy outcome, is trade and dollar policy. The right has pushed a trade (and immigration) agenda over the last three decades that has had the explicit goal of putting non-college-educated workers in direct competition with low-paid workers in the developing world. The predicted and actual effect of this policy is to reduce the wages of non-college-educated workers relative to the wages of more highly educated workers and to increase corporate profits.

The trade deals negotiated over the last three decades have left highly educated workers largely protected from this competition; the agreements mostly focus on subjecting workers without college degrees to international competition. This policy has been carried through under the guise of free trade, but it has nothing to do with promoting free trade: a genuine free trade policy would be designed to place all U.S. workers, not just those without college educations, in competition with their lower-paid counterparts in the developing world.

The value of the dollar is another key policy lever that has been largely kept out of public policy debates. The Federal Reserve Board and the Treasury have enormous ability to influence the value of the dollar. A high dollar makes U.S. goods and services less competitive in the world economy. It makes our exports more expensive to people living in other countries, and it makes imports cheaper for people in the United States. As a result, a high dollar will reduce our exports and increase our imports, creating a trade deficit.

A trade imbalance matters hugely for the distribution of income in a context where some workers are exposed to international competition and others are protected. The high-dollar policy redistributes income from the workers who are exposed to international competition (non-college-educated workers) to those who are largely protected from such competition (primarily highly educated professionals, like doctors and lawyers). The high dollar means that the non-college-educated workers, in the face of competition from lower-cost imports, have to work for less to keep their jobs. On the other hand, those who are protected from this competition keep their good jobs and salaries and get to buy lower-cost imported products.

Is dollar policy just an esoteric, econometric issue? Hardly. Moving the value of the dollar up or down against other currencies by 10 percent has the impact on U.S. employment and wages of a hundred North American Free Trade Agreements. Yet how often might the dollar move that much without a peep from the press or progressive policy makers?

Of course, the hand that controls dollar policy is not the invisible hand of the free market. Business and financial interests have the upper hand at the Treasury Department and the Fed, but almost no one is talking about this important lever of economic power.

Housing policy

Though it is not hard to follow and appreciate Fed policy or the ups and downs of the dollar, we ignore these important economic policies at our peril. Instead, many progressives take the lead of conservatives and focus on the easy-to-see ups and downs of the stock market as a measure of economic health. Yet a mainstream economics textbook would tell us that the value of the stock market is supposed to reflect the value of future corporate profits. Rising profits *could* mean that future growth will be stronger and that wages as well as profits will be higher. On the other hand, the stock market might rise because investors believe that profits will rise at the expense of wages, or as a result of lower corporate tax payments. In the latter, redistributive case, only those who hold lots of stock would have reason to be happy about the prospect of higher stock prices. Higher stock prices ought not to provide any more cause for celebration than higher corn or zinc prices – it's good news for corn and zinc producers, but bad news for everyone else. Thus, there's little benefit from rising stock prices to give progressives cheer.

The same confusion about who benefits extends to rising home prices. Higher home prices do not make society as a whole wealthier; they just increase the share of society's wealth that can be claimed by homeowners. Those who own the most expensive homes are the biggest gainers.

Since homeowners as a group tend to be wealthier than non-homeowners, it is hardly progressive to support the upward redistribution of wealth implied by higher home prices. Higher home prices also have the effect of making it more expensive for current renters to become homeowners. In other words, a policy that leads to higher home prices can be thought of as an unaffordable housing program, a plan for an upward redistribution of income that is 180 degrees at odds with progressive policy.

Most economists, even progressive ones, would no doubt take the arguments presented above in different directions – for example, by arguing that the Fed must restrain employment growth to keep inflation in check, or that patent policy is essential to promote the development of new drugs. But they would not dispute the basic points: the Fed indeed has enormous ability to influence the economy through its control of interest rates and patents are government-granted monopolies that cause drugs and other items to sell for prices far above the free-market price.

If progressives can come to grips with the basic economics of the big issues of the day, then it will at least be possible to make real progress in policy debates. Without this knowledge, it is impossible to even know when progress is being made. When progressives applaud a run-up in the stock market, as many did in the Clinton years, they are rooting for the other team. When progressives devise policies to keep a housing bubble from deflating, they are plotting to use taxpayer dollars to allow the better-off segment of society to benefit at the expense of the less-well-off, the ones who don't own homes or own homes of little value.

The political system and the "free market" are rigged to the advantage of the rich and powerful, which makes it difficult for progressives to make headway in pushing policies that advance the interests of everyone else. However, this mission goes from difficult to achievable if we pay attention to the basic economics. There are enormous obstacles in our path, but if we don't know where we are going, then we can be absolutely sure that we are not going to get there.

Chapter 2

The Economic Crisis:
Where We Are and How We Got Here

There is no cause for progressives to be on the defensive as the United States and most other wealthy countries struggle to recover from the worst downturn since the Great Depression. The economic disaster was entirely the result of conservative economic policies, pursued with reckless abandon. If a progressive government had driven the economy off a similar cliff, progressives could expect to spend at least 40 years in the political wilderness. No one would want to go near such discredited policies.

But progressives *are* on the defensive. A reinvigorated right is openly attacking Social Security and Medicare, looking to take back economic gains that date from the New Deal. It is also doing everything in its power to undermine unions in both the public and private sectors because it recognizes their importance as bulwarks of the Democratic Party and progressive politics more generally. It is even taking steps to roll back the right to vote by pushing measures that will make it more difficult to vote and will explicitly disenfranchise particular groups of people.

How could progressives have allowed themselves to be beaten back? The root of the problem is that President Obama and the leadership of the

Democratic Party backed away from telling the truth about the economic collapse. By refusing to "demonize" Wall Street and the rest of the financial industry for the damage inflicted on the economy and the nation, the president and his party left a huge void that has been filled with alternative stories.

Those who rely on the *Washington Post* and National Public Radio for their news might think that the economy fell into this downturn because reckless government spending sent financial markets into a panic, causing businesses to lay off millions of workers. They are also likely to believe that there will be no hope of recovery until the president and Congress agree on a credible plan to bring spending under control in the decades ahead.

The truth is, this story makes as much sense as blaming the downturn on an attack by space creatures, but in Washington debates it is not necessary that a narrative be grounded in reality. Despite the fact that the budget deficit holds center place in news accounts, it is not the cause of the economy's current problems. The large deficit is rather the result of the economic downturn that began in late 2007, a fact that can be easily shown by examining the Congressional Budget Office's analysis of the budget, as shown in **Figure 2-1**.[5]

Going into the downturn in 2007, the budget deficit was a relatively modest 1.2 percent of GDP, and it was projected to get smaller in the years ahead. It is arguable that even the 2007 deficit was too large – that with the economy near full employment the government should have been running budget surpluses – but it would be a stretch to equate a deficit equal to 1 percent of GDP with runaway borrowing that poses a threat to the government's finances.

The downturn increased the deficit for two reasons. First, government tax revenue and spending responds automatically to a weakening economy. When the economy slows, the government takes in less money in tax revenue. Unemployed workers stop paying Social Security taxes and pay less in income tax. In addition, a higher rate of unemployment means that more money will be paid out in various forms of benefits like food stamps and unemployment insurance. Although budget deficits increase every time we

---

5 The annual budget projections from the Congressional Budget Office, along with regular updates, are available at http://www.cbo.gov/publications/bysubject.cfm?cat=0

have a recession, the increase this time was larger than most because of the severity of the downturn.

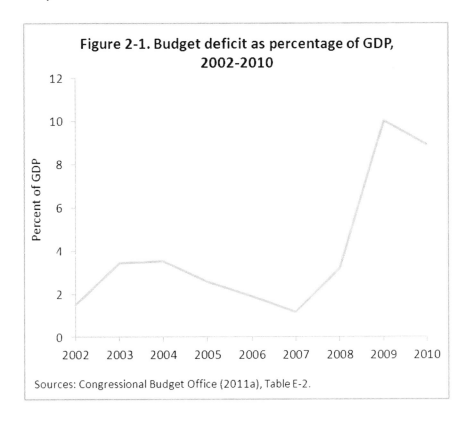

Figure 2-1. Budget deficit as percentage of GDP, 2002-2010

Sources: Congressional Budget Office (2011a), Table E-2.

The other reason that the deficit increased in the downturn was that the government enacted various stimulus packages to boost the economy. It is possible to identify at least three distinct stimulus packages since the downturn began. The first consisted primarily of a tax cut. President Bush signed this package into law in February 2008 at a time when the unemployment rate was just 4.8 percent. President Obama proposed the second package just as he was taking office in January 2009, and Congress approved roughly $700 billion in new tax cuts and additional spending, mostly over calendar years 2009 and 2010.[6] The third stimulus, approved at the end of 2010 at a point when most

---

6 This stimulus package also included roughly $80 billion for a fix to the alternative minimum tax (AMT) that prevented it from raising taxes on millions of middle-income families. This fix really should not be included as part of the stimulus because it is a measure that Congress

of the money from the second stimulus had been spent, extended President Bush's 2001 tax cuts for another two years, reduced the payroll tax by 2 percentage points for a year, and continued extended unemployment benefits through 2011.

These stimulus packages were explicitly designed to offset the effect of reduced private-sector spending. The resulting rise in the deficit stemming from the stimulus packages was not an accident – it was a deliberate goal of the policy. Together the packages added more than $1.5 trillion to the deficits over the fiscal years 2008-2011. However, the spending almost certainly boosted the economy; it increased growth and created jobs.[7] A smaller deficit in these years would have meant slower growth and fewer jobs. In this sense, the deficit is part of the solution, not the problem.

If the deficit were impeding the economy's recovery, it would be through its effect on the interest rate. This is the story of government borrowing pulling money away from the private sector. However, the interest rate on long-term bonds has remained extraordinarily low throughout this period. At the height of the financial crisis, when investors fled to U.S. bonds as a safe asset in a dangerous world, the interest rate on 10-year Treasury bonds hit a low of 2.2 percent. It has remained under 4.0 percent since then and in the summer of 2011 was back down to about 2.2 percent when the threat of the break-up of the euro again panicked financial markets and has been close to 3.0 percent most of the time.

Assuming a 2.0 percent expected inflation rate puts the real interest rate (the actual interest rate minus the inflation rate) at under 2.0 percent and

---

has passed every year for two decades. No one ever expected to pay the higher AMT rate, so preventing this tax increase from going into effect could not have provided a boost to anyone's consumption.

7 See Blinder and Zandi (2010), CBO (2011a), and Feyrer and Sacerdote (2011). It is important to point out that the Feyrer and Sacerdote study almost certainly understates the job impact of the stimulus because it looks exclusively at in-state effects. Much of the employment impact of stimulus spending is likely to spill across state lines. For example, spending on a major construction project in Manhattan is likely to involve subcontractors located in New Jersey. The materials are also likely to come at least in part from out of state. Furthermore, when workers on the project spend their wages, they will be creating jobs in other states if they don't live in New York. For these reasons a study such as this that only picks up the in-state effects will substantially understate the full jobs impact of the stimulus.

often under 1.0 percent for these high-deficit years (**Figure 2-2**). This is a historically low real interest rate that is not consistent with a story of investors panicking over the ability of the U.S. government to repay its debt. When lenders worry about the solvency of their borrowers, they demand real interest rates of 6, 8, or even 10 percent.

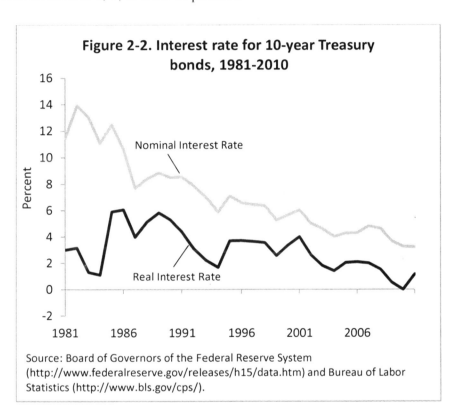

Figure 2-2. Interest rate for 10-year Treasury bonds, 1981-2010

Source: Board of Governors of the Federal Reserve System (http://www.federalreserve.gov/releases/h15/data.htm) and Bureau of Labor Statistics (http://www.bls.gov/cps/).

If investors are willing to hold vast amounts of government bonds at very low interest rates, it is clear that the people who actually have money on the line are not worried about the creditworthiness of the U.S. government, even if the politicians and the pundits are telling them that they should be. In short, the deficit is not the country's problem right now. The problem is a lack of demand, pure and simple. The deficit is hyped as a problem by people who have an alternative agenda of gutting important government social programs, such as Social Security and Medicare.

The cause of the economic crisis:
The collapse of the housing bubble

There continues to be enormous confusion about almost every aspect of the economic crisis. The first point that needs to be clarified is that the main story of the economic crisis was not the financial crisis. The picture of banks collapsing and a chain reaction of defaults and bankruptcies made for exciting news stories and provided the basis for several bestselling books, but this panic was secondary to the collapse of the housing bubble. The housing bubble drove demand in the years since the 2001 recession, and when the trillions of dollars of bubble-generated housing equity disappeared, there was nothing to take its place. This is the complete story of the downturn to date.

The story is not complex or mysterious. It is a simple story that should be widely known, at least by economists, if not the general public. The bubble in housing led to near-record rates of residential construction over the years from 2002 to 2006. Builders rushed to build new homes to take advantage of record-high home prices. The boom also generated an enormous amount of employment in the financial industry, which issued mortgages not just for new homes but also to refinance homes people already owned, as tens of millions of homeowners sought to take advantage of the run-up in prices and low interest rates to take equity out of their homes.

This "housing wealth effect" is well-known and is a standard part of economic theory and modeling. Economists expect households to consume based on their wealth. At its peak, the housing bubble generated more than $8 trillion in home equity on top of what would have been generated had home prices continued to rise at their historic pace. Recent estimates of the size of the wealth effect put it at 6 percent, meaning that homeowners will increase their annual consumption by 6 cents for every additional dollar of home equity.[8] If so, then the equity generated by the housing bubble at its peak in 2006 would have led to almost $500 billion a year in additional consumption.

A bubble in nonresidential real estate led to a building boom in that sector that followed on the heels of the boom in housing; as construction of housing began to trail off at the end of 2005 and into 2006, construction of

---

8 Carroll and Zhou (2010).

nonresidential projects like office buildings, retail malls, and hotels exploded. This boom led to enormous overbuilding in the nonresidential sector, and so when the recession kicked in, and especially after the financial crisis in the fall of 2008, nonresidential construction plummeted.

The impact of the collapse of these two bubbles on the demand for goods and services in the economy was enormous, and continues to be felt. The residential housing sector fell from a peak of 6.2 percent of GDP in 2005 to just 2.2 percent in the first quarter of 2011. The loss of $7 trillion in housing equity (the bubble had not yet fully deflated by the spring of 2011, so there was still about $1 trillion to be lost) led to a sharp fall in consumption. As a result of this lost housing wealth, the savings rate rose from near zero in the years 2004-2007 to over 5 percent by the first quarter of 2009.[9] This corresponds to a loss of more than $500 billion in annual consumption (and reinforces the similar estimate derived from a calculation of the housing wealth effect). It is worth noting that this reduction in spending (and implied increase in savings) has little to do with consumers being pessimistic or wary about the future, though they likely are. Rather, consumers are spending in line with their wealth. Now that their wealth has been hugely reduced by the collapse of the bubble, they have adjusted their spending accordingly.

The overbuilding and collapse of the bubble in nonresidential real estate led to a further loss in annual demand of roughly $250 billion. Adding together the $600 billion in lost residential construction demand (the 4 percentage-point drop in GDP noted above), the $500 billion in lost consumption demand, and the $250 billion in lost demand in nonresidential construction gives a total drop in annual demand of $1.35 trillion.

It didn't end there. State and local governments sought to cut spending and raise taxes when the recession sent their tax collections plummeting. Most state and local governments have balanced-budget requirements, which means that they had no alternative but to raise taxes and cut spending. Their actions had the effect of further reducing demand in the

---

9 The official savings data are somewhat distorted by the mis-measurement of income. Capital gains from the housing market and the stock market appear to have been reported as part of normal income in the government data. (Capital gains are not supposed to count as income in the GDP accounts.) This led to a large shift to a negative statistical discrepancy in the years 2002 to 2007. See Rosnick and Baker (2011b).

economy by roughly $150 billion a year, bringing the total loss of demand in the economy resulting from the collapse of the housing bubble to $1.5 trillion a year.

President Obama's first stimulus package, created to counteract this lost demand, injected roughly $300 billion a year into the economy in calendar years 2009 and 2010 (**Figure 2-3**).[10] It should not be surprising, and dozens of policy makers and economists warned of it at the time, that this stimulus was inadequate to bring the economy back to anything resembling normal levels of employment and output. It simply was not large enough.[11]

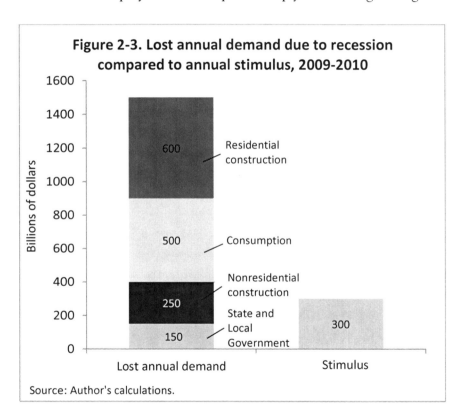

Figure 2-3. Lost annual demand due to recession compared to annual stimulus, 2009-2010

Source: Author's calculations.

The collapse of the real estate bubbles as the cause of our continued economic weakness stands in contrast to the financial crisis stories we keep

---

10 Roughly $100 billion of the stimulus was scheduled to take effect in 2011 or later.
11 For instance, see Baker (2009a), Baker and Deutsch (2009), and Krugman (2009).

reading and hearing about in the news. These stories hinge on the idea that the problem in the economy is the improper working of the financial system following the financial crisis of the fall of 2008. This story has an obvious problem: the reason we have a financial system is to allocate capital, and it doesn't seem that anyone is having difficulty getting capital.

Homebuyers who seek mortgages seem to be getting them; we know this because there has been no appreciable increase in the ratio of mortgage applications to home sales. The Mortgage Bankers Association issues an index every week that tracks the number of mortgage applications received by its members.[12] The banks included in this survey account for well over half of the mortgages issued in the country.

If banks were more hesitant to issue mortgages, we would expect to see the ratio of applications to home purchases skyrocket, because many creditworthy customers would have to make multiple applications just to get a single one approved. Some potential homebuyers would make multiple applications and still not be able to get a mortgage. Since there has been no rise in the ratio of applications to sales, we can assume that access to mortgages is not a big problem in the economy. For the most part, creditworthy homebuyers are still able to get mortgages, generally at historically low interest rates.

There undoubtedly are stricter mortgage standards in place than in the housing bubble years, but this should be expected. During those years, banks issued mortgages whether or not they could be repaid because they were selling them immediately in the secondary market. This is not a sustainable model. It was necessary to return to something resembling the lending patterns of the pre-bubble years.

In the case of businesses, a large portion of corporate America has direct access to credit markets. Large companies routinely go around the banking system by selling bonds and commercial paper directly on credit markets. In this way the United States is fundamentally different from Japan, where banks are far more central in providing finance to the business sector. For this reason, the often-used comparison to Japan's lost decade following the

---

12 The Mortgage Bankers Association index can be found on their website at
    http://www.mortgagebankers.org/.

collapse of its bubbles is inappropriate. Whatever problems may still persist in the banking sector, they are likely to have little impact on the investment and hiring behavior of large corporations.

Looking at the credit markets directly, the interest rates on corporate bonds have been at historically low levels since early in the crisis. From the summer of 2009 through the summer of 2011, the interest rate on high-grade corporate debt was about 5 percent, and the interest rate on Baa debt (lower quality, but still investment grade) averaged less than 6 percent. If we assume a 2 percent average inflation rate going forward, these translate into real rates of 3 percent and 4 percent, respectively – much lower than at most points in the last two decades (**Figure 2-4**). These low rates suggest that large corporations with direct access to credit markets – corporations whose output accounts for close to half of private sector GDP – have had little difficulty obtaining capital. In other words, lack of capital has not been a factor restraining their investment and hiring.

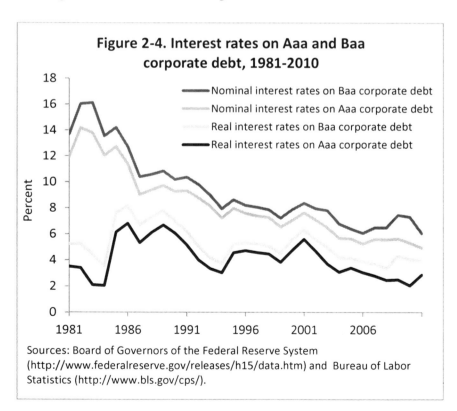

Figure 2-4. Interest rates on Aaa and Baa corporate debt, 1981-2010

Sources: Board of Governors of the Federal Reserve System (http://www.federalreserve.gov/releases/h15/data.htm) and Bureau of Labor Statistics (http://www.bls.gov/cps/).

What about small businesses? If large corporations had access to credit markets but smaller businesses were unable to pursue investment opportunities because they could not get bank credit, then we would expect to see large corporations expanding aggressively in order to gain market share at the expense of their credit-constrained smaller competitors. Yet we see nothing of the sort. Almost all of the major chains, such as Wal-Mart and Starbucks – which would be expected to expand rapidly in this situation – have sharply curtailed their expansion plans in the wake of the downturn. And the reason is weak demand, pure and simple, not any major issues with the banking and financial system.

In any case, access to credit also does not seem to be a problem for small businesses either. The National Federation of Independent Business surveys small business owners to ask what their biggest problem is at the moment. Very few answer that it is difficult for them to borrow money. In the August 2011 survey, 92 percent of small business owners said either that they had ample access to capital or that they had no interest in borrowing.[13] The biggest problem cited by these small business owners was "poor sales" – in other words, inadequate demand.

In addition, business investment in equipment and software has actually held up fairly well in this downturn, suggesting that access to capital is not the problem. **Figure 2-5** shows investment in equipment and software as a share of GDP over the last decade. While the levels reached at the end of 2010 and the start of 2011 are still below their pre-recession levels, they are surprisingly high given the large amounts of excess capacity in most sectors of the economy.

---

13 Dunkelberg and Wade (2011).

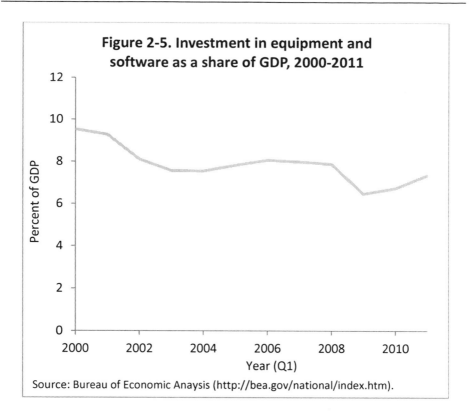

Figure 2-5. Investment in equipment and software as a share of GDP, 2000-2011

Source: Bureau of Economic Anaysis (http://bea.gov/national/index.htm).

We also hear over and over again the claim that uncertainty about tax or regulatory policy is impeding hiring and causing continued economic weakness. If this were true, we would expect to see firms increasing average hours per worker and/or hiring more temporary workers to meet demand. Through these strategies, firms could get more labor without making the commitment to hiring new permanent employees.

Yet there is no evidence of either trend in the economy. While average weekly hours have risen slightly from their low point of the downturn (from 33.7 hours per week in June 2009 to 34.4 in June 2011), the average work week is still below its pre-recession peak of 34.7 hours per week. The uptick in average weekly hours thus far has been fairly typical of what would be expected in a recovery. The same applies to the hiring of temporary employees. Temporary employment fell by more than 30 percent at the start of the downturn, as firms reduced the number of temporary workers by more than 800,000. Less than 500,000 of these workers have been rehired thus far in the upturn, leaving temporary employment almost 13 percent below its pre-recession level.[14]

Moreover, if uncertainty about regulations and taxes were a major factor impeding hiring, then its impact should be uneven between sectors with high and low turnover. In sectors with high turnover, like retail and restaurants, it is difficult to see how regulatory uncertainty could be an issue, since firms could quickly get back to their desired employment level through attrition. This would mean that, if the economy were fine and the problem was regulation, we should expect to see high-turnover sectors growing rapidly, while sectors with low turnover, like manufacturing, would have very slow employment growth. There is no evidence of this sort of shift in job gains in the recovery, providing yet another reason for rejecting the argument that uncertainty about the future is a serious factor slowing employment growth.[15]

In short, the basic story of the economic downturn approximately four years after the start of the Great Recession is a simple one. The economy suffers from a shortfall in demand. Whatever problems may persist in the financial system are not substantially impeding growth. Larger firms have little difficulty getting access to capital at historically low interest rates. Smaller firms do not identify access to capital as one of their biggest problems. And homebuyers appear undeterred in their attempts to secure mortgages.

Finally, it is worth putting to rest one of the most pervasive myths that came out of the worst days of the financial crisis in late 2008 and early 2009. This myth is that the country was saved from the risk of a second Great Depression only by the quick action of the Fed and the Treasury.

According to the story, the lending approved by Congress in the Troubled Asset Relief Program (TARP) along with special lending facilities created by the Federal Reserve Board prevented a financial collapse that would have precipitated another Great Depression. While these measures deserve credit for preventing a financial collapse, there is no reason to believe that a

---

14 These numbers refer to the somewhat larger "employment services" category that includes temporary help agencies as well as some employment leasing services that are not included in this category.

15 It is also worth noting that the NFIB shows no rise in the percentage of firms that list regulation and taxes as major problem compared with the Bush presidency.

financial collapse would have led to a second Great Depression, defined as a decade of double-digit unemployment.

The first Great Depression was not just the result of mismanagement of a banking crisis in its early days. The failure of the Fed and the Treasury to take steps to backstop the banking system undoubtedly led to a more severe downturn for the economy and to financial disasters for millions of families who lost their life's savings in failed banks. However, nothing about this initial failure to act decisively doomed the economy to a decade of double-digit unemployment. Rather, the extended depression was the result of persistent policy failures over the course of a decade.

The United States ultimately emerged from the depression as a result of the massive deficit spending associated with World War II. The spending associated with the war can be seen as a beneficial accident from the standpoint of an economy that desperately needed a massive dose of government stimulus. However, nothing in principle would have prevented massive government spending for domestic reconstruction efforts at a much earlier point. In other words, there was no economic reason that the government could not have made the same commitment in terms of spending and hiring for projects to rebuild the country's infrastructure, to build up its housing stock, and to improve education and training that it eventually made to fight World War II. Had it made this commitment in 1931 rather than 1941, the government would have spared the country a decade of depression.

This sort of increase in spending could have pulled the country out the Great Depression at any point after the initial financial crisis. The obstacles to going this route were political, not economic. The same would have been the case had the financial crisis in 2008 actually led to the collapse of the financial system and the need to pick up the pieces from scratch. Today, having learned the lessons from World War II, we know how to reflate the economy. While a full-scale financial collapse – with the destruction of tens of trillions of dollars of wealth overnight – would be devastating to the economy and the people who suffer the losses, it would take a decade of failed policy in addition to this collapse to give us a second Great Depression. There is no reason to believe that the country would have repeated the policy mistakes of the thirties even if the Fed and the Treasury had failed to check the financial panic at the start of the crisis.

This point is relevant in terms of how we view the conduct of the Bush and Obama administrations and the Fed under Chairman Ben Bernanke. If it is really the case that a second Great Depression was only narrowly averted, then we all should be grateful, even if the cost was to largely leave the financial system in place, with the too-big-to-fail banks even bigger than they were before the crisis. After all, giving taxpayer money to the top management and shareholders of Citigroup, Goldman Sachs, and Morgan Stanley is a price worth paying if it was necessary to prevent a second Great Depression.[16] However, such handouts may look different if even the worst-case scenario did not look anything like the Great Depression.

We have high unemployment because we lack the political will to get the economy moving again

We know how to get out of this trough: we need to spend much more money. However, the current political situation precludes this option. Politicians and the national media have become fixated on reducing the budget deficit and have largely decided to ignore the problem of unemployment and underemployment.

In the current political environment it is somehow responsible to push spending cuts, even though the main impact of these cuts is to slow the economy and raise the unemployment rate further. But logic has little place right now in national policy debates, just as arithmetic played little role in economic policy in the buildup of the housing bubble.

---

16 It is worth noting again that taxpayers gifted tens of billions of dollars to the financial industry despite the oft-repeated claim that the government made money on TARP and the special lending facilities. The money that the government lent to banks like Goldman Sachs and Citigroup was made available at interest rates far below what the banks would have been required to pay in the market at the time. In the case of Goldman Sachs and Morgan Stanley, the two surviving independent investment banks, the Fed allowed them to change their status in the middle of the crisis to bank holding companies that had the protection of the Fed and the Federal Deposit Insurance Corporation. This change effectively told the markets that these huge institutions would be backstopped by the government, bringing to an end a run on both banks. An enormous premium was placed on liquidity at the time of TARP. The fact that the major Wall Street banks were able to borrow at near zero rates, at a time when they were insolvent and would have found it almost impossible to get private-sector loans at any price, was an enormous subsidy.

Deficit reduction has become an end in itself. In this scenario, "serious people" propose large spending cuts, but only "crazy ideologues" talk about measures that would boost economic growth and reduce unemployment.

Chapter 3

The Great Redistribution

The U.S. economy has been driven by asset bubbles since the mid-1990s, but this is not the ordinary source of our economic growth. In the three decades following World War II, the economy had strong growth driven by wage-led consumption. Throughout this period, productivity growth translated into wage growth at all points along the income ladder. Those at the bottom saw their wages and income rise as fast, or faster, than those at the top. This created self-sustaining growth, since most workers spent most of their income and ensured that demand kept pace with productivity growth. Firms would then invest in new plant and equipment, which would lead to further increases in productivity, and in turn to additional wage growth.

Apart from some brief recessions, this cycle continued until it was derailed by the oil price shocks of the 1970s. The price of oil more than tripled between 1972 and 1975, shaking an economy that was already facing high inflation. Then, during the Iranian revolution at the end of the decade, oil prices rose by more than 150 percent.[17] Both shocks coincided with, and

---

17 At the time, Iran was the world's second-largest exporter of oil, and the revolution removed these exports from world markets. For a history of oil prices in the post-World War II era see
http://www.inflationdata.com/inflation/inflation_rate/historical_oil_prices_table.asp.

possibly caused, a sharp slowdown in productivity growth that, combined with high inflation, brought an end to the period of broadly shared growth of the prior three decades.

When President Reagan took office in 1981, he had an explicit policy of putting the country on a different sort of growth path, and he largely succeeded. While President Reagan's tax cuts – which disproportionately benefited higher-income taxpayers – are widely remembered, they are the less important part of the story. The upward redistribution of before-tax income in the years since 1980 has had far more impact on inequality and the living standards of the bulk of the population than the changes toward a more regressive system of taxation.

Making money flow upward

This upward redistribution was not the result of the natural workings of the market. President Reagan and his successors put in place a variety of measures that had the effect of weakening the bargaining power of ordinary workers. Together these measures had the effect of driving down the wages of those at the middle and the bottom of the income distribution, to the benefit of those at the top.

Heading this list of policy changes was the tighter monetary policy pursued by the Federal Reserve Board in the years after 1980. Fighting inflation became the Fed's overwhelming concern, and it was willing to tolerate high unemployment rates to reduce inflation to levels it considered acceptable. This was clearly demonstrated by Paul Volcker in 1982 when he pushed the unemployment rate to almost 11 percent in order to rein in inflation. His successor, Alan Greenspan, was similarly committed to low inflation. The modest acceleration in the inflation rate at the end of the 1980s was sufficient to prompt a round of interest rate hikes that eventually led to the 1990-1991 recession. The current Fed chairman, Ben Bernanke, has committed the Fed to a 2.0 percent inflation ceiling, implying that he would raise interest rates and push up unemployment if he believed that core inflation might exceed this level.

This focus on inflation represents a sharp shift from the Fed's policy in prior decades. While the Fed was always concerned about inflation and had brought on recessions in the past as part of its effort to control it, Volcker began a new era in which fighting inflation became a much greater priority than sustaining high employment, the other half of the Fed's mandate.

The policy of raising unemployment to fight inflation has the effect of redistributing income upward because it is overwhelmingly less-educated workers who lose their jobs when the unemployment rate rises. The unemployment rate for all categories of workers rises during a recession, but the largest increases will be for workers with less education. The percentage of factory workers and retail clerks who lose their job in a downturn is far higher than the percentage of doctors and lawyers. As a result, the workers who end up taking the biggest pay cuts in a downturn are those without college degrees and especially those without high school degrees.[18]

High unemployment is a class-biased mechanism for fighting inflation. In effect it forces the less-advantaged groups in society to sacrifice to ensure that the more-advantaged can enjoy price stability – and a ready supply of low-cost labor to provide household help or serve them in hotels and restaurants.

Weakening unions

As another element of this process of upward redistribution, President Reagan took a number of steps to weaken the power of unions. Foremost was weakening the enforcement of labor laws that protect workers' right to organize. While labor laws that protect management are still vigorously enforced (a union engaged in a secondary strike[19] can expect to have its officers jailed and its bank accounts seized), the enforcement of rules protecting the right to organize has become a joke. Employers routinely fire workers for organizing[20] and they know that they are unlikely to lose a case at the National

---

18 The differential effect of unemployment on the wages of less-highly paid workers is discussed in Bernstein and Baker (2004).

19 Also known as a "secondary boycott," a secondary strike is "an attempt to stop others from purchasing products from, performing services for, or otherwise doing business with a company that does business with another company that is in the midst of a labor dispute." See http://www.nolo.com/dictionary/secondary-boycott-term.html.

20 Schmitt and Zipperer (2009).

Labor Relations Board (NLRB) or that in any case penalties will be inconsequential.

The Reagan administration not only placed more management-friendly officials in the NLRB, it also deliberately underfunded the board, allowing an enormous backlog of complaints to build. At its worst, the backlog was more than two years, meaning that employees fired during an organizing drive might have to wait more than two years before they could have a hearing. In this case, even if the NLRB ruled for the workers and gave them their jobs back, any organizing drive in which they had participated would almost certainly be long over.

The strike as a weapon to protect workers' rights has become less effective because employers now routinely hire replacement workers. This became a common practice in the private sector after President Reagan fired the air traffic controllers who went on strike in the summer of 1981. While the strike was illegal and Reagan had the authority to fire and replace striking workers, until then the usual practice at all levels of government had been to try to reach an accommodation with striking workers.

Major firms in the private sector – notably Eastern Airlines and Greyhound – quickly emulated Reagan's hard-line stance. In the wake of the controllers' strike, hiring replacements became a standard response to strikes and seriously reduced the value of strikes as a union weapon. The fact that there are large numbers of potential replacement workers readily available for hire is the result of both the sharp decline in unionization rates over the last three decades and also the difficulty that most workers have in finding decent-paying jobs.

Deregulation of major sectors like airlines, trucking, and telecommunications was another route to weaken labor unions. Together the transportation and utility sectors employed more than 6.4 million workers in 1979, 8.6 percent of the private-sector workforce.[21] Prior to deregulation (which began in the Carter administration), these sectors were heavily unionized, with workers sharing in the gains from the protection that regulation afforded. Deregulation both opened these sectors to non-union competitors and also put serious pressure on the wages of workers in the

21 Bureau of the Census (1980), Table 679.

unionized firms that survived. While there were clear benefits to deregulation in these industries, one of the major outcomes was a sharp reduction in the size of the unionized workforce.

Together these policies had the effect of sending the unionization rate in the private sector plummeting. It had been close to 20 percent in 1980 when Reagan took office, but it was down to 12 percent by 1990, had fallen to 9 percent in 2000, and was below 7 percent in 2010.[22] This drop in the unionization rate not only weakened the bargaining power of non-college-educated workers, but it also substantially reduced their political power.[23] In political campaigns, unions had been an effective counterweight to corporate interests and the interests of the wealthy more generally. As their membership has declined over the last three decades, they have become less able to play this role.

The high-dollar policy

The high dollar, coupled with U.S. trade policies of the last three decades, is also an important tool for redistributing income upward. A conscious goal of trade agreements like the North American Free Trade Agreement (NAFTA) is to make it as easy as possible for U.S. manufacturers to relocate their operations to Mexico and other developing countries. This has the effect of putting U.S. manufacturing workers in direct competition with low-paid workers in the developing world. The predicted and actual result of this policy is to eliminate jobs in manufacturing in the U.S. and to put downward pressure on the wages of the workers still employed in the sector.

It is important to realize that these deals have nothing to do with free trade, even though all the pacts are called free trade agreements to make them sound more appealing to the general public, or at least to the pundits who like to think of themselves as supporters of free trade. These agreements do little to undermine the legal and professional barriers that protect highly educated

---

22 Reinhold (2000) and Bureau of Labor Statistics.

23 While many college-educated workers and even workers with advanced degrees are unionized, unionization leads to much larger wage gains for less-educated workers (Schmitt, 2008).

professionals from competing with their lower-paid counterparts in the developing world.

Just as trade models show that U.S. consumers can benefit from having work performed by low-paid manufacturing workers in the developing world, the same models show that U.S. consumers can benefit from having access to low-paid professionals from the developing world. The developing world has an enormous pool of highly educated workers, some of whom are already trained to U.S. standards, and many more of whom could and would be trained to U.S. standards, if there were a reason. Because these workers live in countries that are much poorer than the United States, they would be willing to work for wages that are far lower than their professional counterparts here, just as in the case of manufacturing workers in the developing world.

However, free-trade agreements are not designed to free trade in professional services. In drafting NAFTA, U.S. trade negotiators eagerly sought out the opinion of manufacturers, asking them to identify obstacles that prevented them from relocating operations to Mexico and other developing countries, but there was no comparable outreach to hospital administrators or law firms to determine the barriers that prevented them from hiring low-paid (but highly qualified) doctors and lawyers from India or Mexico. This apparent discrepancy was again the result of a conscious decision to design policy in a way that redistributes income upward.

The impact of current trade policy is amplified by the overvaluation of the dollar. A higher-valued dollar makes U.S. exports more expensive to the rest of world and makes imports from abroad cheaper for people living in the United States. These price differences increase the downward pressure on the wages for workers in sectors subject to international competition while actually benefiting those who are protected, since the latter will be able to buy imported goods more cheaply. Over most of the period since 1980 the United States has had an overvalued dollar, often quite deliberately, further contributing to the downward pressure on the wages of less-educated workers.

Many large manufacturers were pushed to the edge of bankruptcy or beyond in the mid-1980s, the first period of major dollar overvaluation. Millions of manufacturing jobs disappeared in the late 1990s and 2000s, even before the recession, as a result of a second surge in the value of the dollar starting in 1997. This has all had the effect of weakening unions – once heavily concentrated in manufacturing – and putting downward pressure on wages in major sectors such as the auto and steel industry.

Corporate governance

The rules on corporate governance also play an important role in the upward redistribution of income. As the practice stands now, the top management of major corporations is in a position to pick the board of directors, who then decide the salaries of top management. To ensure that directors will be loyal, they are offered annual compensation in the hundreds of thousands of dollars to attend four to eight meetings a year. Few directors will jeopardize such a plush deal by making an issue out of management pay. Of course, likely troublemakers are unlikely to be picked for a board in the first place.

The result is that top corporate management in the United States has come to be paid far more than its counterparts in Europe and Asia, primarily over the last three decades. Essentially, the structures (either dominant shareholders or social norms) that had previously placed a check on the pay of top management broke down. With no policy response to create new checks on management pay, top managers have been freed to write their own paychecks at the expense of the employees, shareholders and other corporate stakeholders.

Patent monopolies

Finally, the number of patents has exploded in the last three decades, as patent protection has become both easier to obtain and stronger. Patent monopolies allow firms to charge far more than the competitive market price for their products. This price advantage can be seen most clearly in the case of prescription drugs. In 2010, spending on prescription drugs amounted to almost 2 percent of GDP, compared to less than half a percent in 1980. The higher expenditures are almost entirely a function of patent protection. Then, as now, drugs are cheap to produce, and it is only patent monopolies that make them expensive to buy.

The main beneficiaries of patent protection are invariably more highly educated workers. A recent study of wealthy countries by the Organization for Economic Cooperation and Development (OECD) found that the number of patents per capita was the most important factor determining the extent to which income was redistributed upward from those at the middle and bottom to those at the top over the last three decades.[24]

Wage-led versus bubble-driven consumption

The upward redistribution of income since the early 1980s laid the basis for the bubble economy. This can be seen by looking at two important implications for the larger economy which had resulted from the broad sharing of the benefits of productivity growth in the three decades after World War II. First, since most workers could be counted on to spend most of their income, the pattern of distribution ensured that demand would keep pace with productivity growth. The income generated by productivity growth was spent rather than saved. When ordinary workers stopped sharing in the gains of productivity growth, inadequate demand became a problem.

The second implication was that rising wages could lead to inflationary pressures. If wages generally rise in step with productivity growth, there is always a risk that wages will occasionally outstrip it. For example, if a contract provides for real wage increases of 2 percent, but productivity growth is only 1 percent, firms will either see a reduction in profit margins or be forced to raise their prices by more than the overall inflation rate. This response can lead to the sort of wage-price spiral the country experienced in the 1970s, when productivity growth lagged real wage growth for a short period.

However, in a climate where workers have considerably little bargaining power, a wage-price spiral is a less serious threat. This diminished risk was the reason Alan Greenspan felt so comfortable in the 1990s with allowing interest rates to remain low and for the unemployment rate to fall to levels unseen since the 1960s. With the weak bargaining position of workers in the 1990s, inflation simply was not a problem, and Greenspan was an astute

---

24 OECD (2011).

enough observer of the economy (unlike most academic economists) to recognize this fact.

Low interest rates have a positive but limited impact in increasing demand. They do lead to somewhat higher investment, but a large body of research shows that investment is not very responsive to lower interest rates. Low interest rates can lead to a fall in the dollar, which would boost net exports, but there were other factors keeping the dollar high during this period. In fact, the main effect of the low interest rates sustained through the late 1990s and the 2000s was to create the possibility for the bubble economy, the dynamics of which are explored in the next chapter.

Chapter 4

The Bubble Economy

There is a frequently told tale in Washington of the 1990s prosperity, and Bill Clinton is its hero. In this story, President Clinton performed the hard work of bringing down the deficit and balancing the budget. He raised taxes and contained spending, but the pain was rewarded by low interest rates and a growth boom that delivered the lowest unemployment rates in more than three decades. It's a great morality tale, but it has little to do with the actual economic history of the decade.

During the first half of the Clinton era, the economy experienced very modest growth. Workers saw little benefit because wages were essentially stagnant. Then, in the late 1990s, a stock bubble emerged, and growth took off and real wages started to rise. This extraordinary period of bubble-driven growth was the main factor in flipping the government's budget from deficits to surpluses.

The Congressional Budget Office's (CBO) projections from May 1996 (after all the tax increases and spending cuts had been put into law) showed the government running a deficit of 2.7 percent of GDP in 2000. Instead, that year saw a surplus equal to 2.1 percent of GDP, which translated into a shift from deficit to surplus of more than 5 percentage points of GDP (about $750 billion in 2011 dollars). Not one dollar of this shift was attributable to fiscal restraint. According to CBO, the net effect of legislated changes over this period was to *increase* the fiscal year 2000 deficit by $10 billion (**Figure 4-1**). Rather than higher taxes or spending cuts, the entire cause of the shift from deficit to surplus was better-than-expected growth and lower-than-expected unemployment. In its 1996 projections, CBO assumed that the unemployment rate would be 6.0 percent in 2000, which was its estimate of the non-accelerating inflation rate of unemployment (NAIRU) at the time. It was only because the stock bubble drove demand much faster than expected, and Fed Chairman Alan Greenspan allowed the unemployment rate to fall below the generally accepted estimates of the NAIRU, that the deficit turned into a surplus.

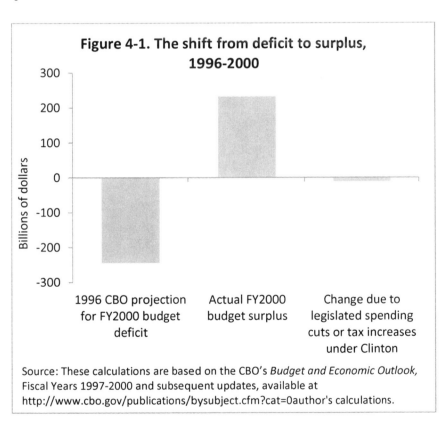

Figure 4-1. The shift from deficit to surplus, 1996-2000

Source: These calculations are based on the CBO's *Budget and Economic Outlook, Fiscal Years 1997-2000* and subsequent updates, available at http://www.cbo.gov/publications/bysubject.cfm?cat=0author's calculations.

There is another important chapter of the Clinton morality tale that turns out to be more fiction than fact. Nominal interest rates indeed fell, but the decline in the real interest rate from the high-deficit years of the 1980s was quite modest. And the small decline had little effect on investment. The investment share of GDP at its peak in the 1990s cycle (which was in 2000) was somewhat higher than it had been in the 1980s but was still below its 1970s' peak (**Figure 4-2**).[25] Furthermore, the uptick in productivity growth in the 1990s, which many associate with an "investment boom," began before investment had recovered even to the 1980s level.

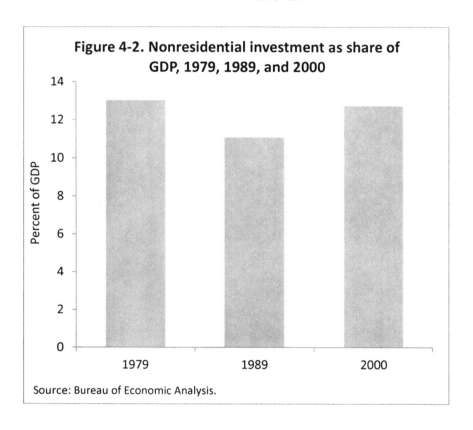

Figure 4-2. Nonresidential investment as share of GDP, 1979, 1989, and 2000

Source: Bureau of Economic Analysis.

---

25 It's worth noting that about 0.3 percentage points of the increase in investment in the 1990s is simply an accounting issue. There was a huge expansion of car leasing in the decade. A leased car counts as investment on the part of the car leasing company. By contrast, if a person buys a car it counts as consumption. The shift from purchases to leases increased annual investment by an amount equal to 0.3 percent of GDP at the end of the decade.

In short, the good economic news in the 1990s had little to do with the deficit reduction measures of the Clinton administration. The fuel for the business cycle was consumption, not investment, which was in turn the result of the wealth effect attributable to $10 trillion of stock bubble wealth. This ephemeral wealth increased annual consumption by $300-400 billion a year, or 3 to 4 percent of GDP. The household savings rate fell to what were at the time record lows. Net national savings actually hit their lowest levels of the postwar period, in spite of the large budget surpluses at the end of the decade. In fact, the switch from federal deficits to surpluses was more than offset by a reduction in private-sector savings. By the end of the decade, the country was engaged in large-scale borrowing from abroad, even as it was running huge budget surpluses.

The overvalued dollar of the Clinton era

If the story of the virtues of President Clinton's fiscal austerity is often oversold, the story of his overvaluation of the dollar is rarely told at all. A major part of the standard story of deficit reduction is supposed to be a decline in the value of the dollar. The lower interest rates that result from reduced government borrowing are supposed to make it less attractive for foreign investors to hold dollar-denominated assets, like government bonds and the bonds of private corporations. If foreign investors buy fewer dollar assets, then the value of the dollar should fall relative to the value of other currencies.

This is a good outcome in the context of deficit reduction because a lower-valued dollar makes our exports cheaper for people living in other countries, and so they buy more of them. A lower-valued dollar will also make imports more expensive for people living in the United States, leading us to buy fewer imports and more domestically produced goods. The result is that we export more and import less, thereby reducing the trade deficit and possibly even turning it into a surplus.

In the first half of the Clinton administration, to some extent, this process played out as the textbook would dictate, but the tables turned when Robert Rubin became Treasury Secretary in January 1995. Rubin was openly committed to a strong dollar. When he first took office this may have just been words, but in 1997, during the East Asian financial crisis, he had the opportunity to put some serious muscle behind them.

The United States used its de-facto control of the International Monetary Fund (IMF) to impose harsh conditions on the crisis countries. The IMF effectively acted as an enforcement agent for the banks that had made loans to the companies and countries in the region. To repay these loans, the countries had to run massive trade surpluses, which required a sharp decline in the value of their currencies against the dollar in order to make their exports hypercompetitive and to discourage imports.

The impact of the IMF's policies extended well beyond the countries directly affected by the crisis. Other developing countries took their cue from the experience of East Asia and realized that they did not want to be in a similar situation where they might be forced to turn to the IMF for assistance. Protecting themselves meant accumulating huge amounts of currency reserves as an insurance policy. And the way to accumulate reserves is to run large trade surpluses. This in turn means lowering the value of your currency relative to the dollar.

These moves gave Robert Rubin the strong dollar he wanted. A strong dollar helped to keep inflation low by keeping import prices down. It also meant running a huge trade deficit, an inevitable result of an overvalued dollar. At the end of the Clinton boom, the U.S. economy was fueled by an unsustainable stock bubble and was running an unsustainable trade deficit. Neither was good long-term policy, but together they created several years of prosperity in which unemployment fell to lower levels than most economists thought possible, and most workers experienced healthy wage growth.

The end of the stock bubble and the 2001 recession

Bubbles inevitably burst, and the stock bubble in the United States did so in dramatic fashion beginning in 2000. The tech sector was the leading edge of the bubble; it had seen the biggest run-up and eventually endured the deepest plunge.[26] The NASDAQ, which is dominated by relatively new firms in the

---

26 The bubble is often referred to as the "tech bubble" or the "internet bubble," implying that it was restricted to a narrow category of the stock market. While these sectors were most

tech sector, rose from 925 at the end of 1995 to 3740 at the end of 1999. After peaking at 5148 in March 2000, it fell below 4000 by the summer. It had some further ups and downs, but it eventually bottomed out at just over 1100 in September 2002, losing more than 75 percent of its value.

The stock market plunge affected the economy in two ways. First, the bubble years were extraordinary in that they were a period in which firms sold stock on a large scale to finance new investment. (More typically new firms sell off stock to allow entrepreneurs to cash out some of their profits, whereas older firms sell off stock to pay down debt.) However, the plunge in the market ended this channel of investment finance. Investment fell by 14.2 percent between the fourth quarter of 2000 and its bottom in the first quarter of 2003.

The more important channel through which the plunge in the market affected the economy was through its impact on consumption. The savings rate had fallen to 2.9 percent at the peak of the bubble in 2000. The destruction of $10 trillion in paper wealth would theoretically lead to a reduction in annual consumption of $300-400 billion, as mentioned above. Consumption did in fact fall sharply in response to the drop in the stock market. The adjusted savings rate rose by roughly 3 percentage points between 2000 and 2002, corresponding to a drop in annual consumption of more than $250 billion.[27]

The result of the drop in investment and the fall in consumption due to the wealth effect was the 2001 recession. Officially and by most accounts this recession was short and mild; it is dated as running from March to December 2001, almost as short as a recession can possibly be. However, the economy had considerable difficulty recovering from it. Job losses continued

---

affected by the bubble, virtually all sectors of the market saw substantial price increases during the inflation of the bubble and experienced substantial declines when it burst. For example, Ford's stock rose from under $29 in late 1995 to a peak of more than $63 in early 1999. It eventually fell below $9 in the fall of 2002. McDonald's stock rose from under $20 in the summer of 1995 to a peak of more than $45 in early 1999, and it eventually fell to under $15 in early 2003.

27 The adjusted savings rate adds the statistical discrepancy in the national income accounts to income, under the assumption that most of the change in the statistical discrepancy through time is attributable to capital gains income showing up as normal income (Rosnick and Baker, 2011b). This explains the fact that the statistical discrepancy shifted from being positive through most of the postwar period to being a large negative at the peaks of the stock and housing bubbles.

through 2002, and the economy didn't start creating jobs again until September 2003. It was not until February 2005 that the economy finally regained all the jobs it lost during the recession. Until the current downturn, this was the longest stretch that the United States had gone without creating jobs since the Great Depression.

The recovery was slow and weak because the 2001 downturn was not like prior postwar recessions. The Federal Reserve Board had engineered the previous recessions by raising interest rates to combat inflation. The intention of higher rates was to slow the economy through reduced demand for interest-sensitive items, like houses and cars. When demand fell, growth would slow, leading to fewer jobs. Fewer jobs translate into a higher unemployment rate, which in turns puts downward pressure on wages, thereby alleviating the threat of inflation. This is the standard Fed formula.

When the Fed determines that the threat of inflation has been eliminated, it lowers rates again. Since the recession period of high interest rates creates pent-up demand for housing and cars, the lowering of interest rates usually triggers a flurry of home buying and new construction as well as a surge of car sales.

However, this was not the story in the 2001 recession. The recession was the result not of the Fed raising interest rates but of the collapse of the stock bubble. Thus, there was no pent-up demand to be triggered by a decline in interest rates. The Fed did push the overnight federal funds rate down to 1.0 percent, the lowest level since the early 1950s, but the response was limited.

It is worth emphasizing how constrained the Fed was at this time. It had not pushed the federal funds rate below 3.0 percent since the early 1960s, so the 1.0 percent rate was truly extraordinary. For practical purposes, the federal funds rate was pretty much at its lower bound, since the marginal impact of going all the way down to zero from 1.0 percent is likely to be minimal. The European Central Bank has never lowered its overnight rate below 1.0 percent in the post-2007 downturn even though it engaged in quantitative easing and other extraordinary measures to boost the economy.

The Fed's response to the 2001 downturn belies the notion that the recession was short and mild. Though that may have been the case officially, and the unemployment rate did not rise strongly, the consequences for the economy and especially the labor market were severe.

One aspect of the weak recovery is the pattern followed by the trade deficit. Usually the trade deficit shrinks in a downturn, as the country buys fewer imports along with less of everything else. The trade deficit declined modestly in 2001, but it began to rise rapidly in 2002 and continued to rise until 2006. This outcome was more fallout from the overvalued dollar.

The turnaround that eventually allowed the economy to grow fast enough to create jobs was primarily due to the growth of the housing bubble. Like the alcoholic who recovers from the effects of a hangover by drinking again in the morning, the economy used the growth generated by the housing bubble to recover from the collapse of the stock bubble.

By 2002 it was already possible to recognize that the housing market was in a bubble.[28] In the years since 1996, home prices had risen by more than 30 percent after adjusting for inflation. This rise followed a 100-year trend in which nationwide home prices had just tracked the overall rate of inflation.[29] The U.S. housing market was valued at more than $14 trillion in 2002, making it the largest market in the world. When there is a longstanding trend in an enormous market, it is reasonable to expect it to persist unless some large change in the fundamentals justifies a departure from the trend.

A quick examination of the fundamentals showed there to be no plausible explanation for the sharp run-up in prices. On the demand side, neither population growth nor income growth provided helpful explanations. Population growth had actually slowed considerably from prior periods. It might have been reasonable to expect some pressure on home prices when the huge baby boom cohort was first forming its own households, but this would have occurred in the 1970s and 1980s, not 2002, when the youngest baby boomer was already 38 and the oldest was 54.

The story on the income side was no better. The country had experienced healthy income growth in the late 1990s, but it was not

---

28 The evidence is laid out in Baker (2002b).

29 The existence of a 100-year-long trend was uncovered in research by Robert Shiller (2006), which was not yet available in 2002. However, it was possible to use publicly available data sources to determine that nationwide home prices had just tracked inflation since 1953 (see Baker 2002b).

extraordinary – no better than the average income growth the country had experienced over the long boom from 1947 to 1973. Home prices had already increased in real terms over that period, and so there is no reason to expect that four years of good growth in the late 1990s would lead to a 30 percent rise in home prices. Furthermore, the recession in 2001 brought this income growth to an end, with real incomes flat or declining subsequently, yet home prices continued to rise.

The supply side also offered no plausible explanations. In testimony before Congress in 2002, the Federal Reserve Board chairman commented on the run-up in home prices and mentioned the limited supply of available land and environmental restrictions on building. [30] Neither of these seemed plausible as explanations for an increase in home prices beginning in the mid-1990s. There had always been a limited supply of land in especially attractive places to live; this was not a new feature of the housing bubble. As far as environmental restrictions on building, Republicans had taken over Congress in 1994 (and many state houses as well), so the late 1990s could hardly be viewed as the heyday of environmental legislation. Furthermore, it was only necessary to look at the data on construction, which showed housing starts at a near-record rate. While there may have been obstacles to building, they were not impeding supply in any important way.

Lacking any explanation for the price run-up on either the supply or demand side of the market, it was also possible to turn to rents for evidence that fundamentals were not responsible for the rise in home prices. If the rise were being driven by the fundamentals of the housing market, there should be a comparable increase in rents, since owning and renting are loose substitutes. If the fundamentals of the housing market were driving up sales prices, then they should also be driving up rents. But rents showed no remotely comparable rise. They did outpace the overall inflation rate by about 1 percentage point annually from 1996 to 2000, but from that point forward they were flat in real terms until the bubble finally burst. This should have been a big warning sign that the run-up in prices was driven by a bubble. [31] One

---

30 Greenspan (2002).

31 There was the possibility that the gap between home sale prices and rent was driven by the extraordinarily low mortgage rates available at the time. This argument has two problems.

other item that economists could have checked to determine whether home prices were driven by fundamentals was the vacancy rate. The Census Bureau publishes data on vacancy rates every quarter,[32] and these data are a very basic measure of the slack in the housing market. If the run-up in home prices had been due to a shortage of housing, then vacancy rates ought to have been at very low levels. In fact, the opposite was true: the vacancy rate had already hit a record high by 2002 (and it continued to rise through the later bubble years).

The fact that the big increase in vacancies was in rental units, not ownership units, still reflected an excess supply of housing that could be expected to exert downward pressure on rents, which would in turn also put downward pressure on sale prices as people opted to take advantage of cheap rents rather than buying. In addition, if rents are falling while sale prices are rising, landlords will convert rental units into ownership units. This can be costly in some cases (many cities have laws protecting renters from being displaced), but if the gains are large enough, landlords can and do find ways to make these conversions. Furthermore, almost a third of rental units are single-family homes that require little work to convert to ownership units.

In sum, by 2002 the housing market was experiencing a bubble that should have been apparent to policy makers. Instead, all the people in top policy-making positions ignored the evidence and insisted that everything was fine with the housing market and the economy.

First, home prices have not historically been very sensitive to interest rates, and for prices to fluctuate in major ways as interest rates moved up or down would amount to a sharp break with past patterns. The other, more important, problem with this story is that no one expected interest rates to remain at such low levels. If it was the case that the extraordinary run-up in home prices was due to the unusually low interest rates available at the time, then one would expect home prices to fall back to their trend level when interest rates rose back to more normal levels. Rather than being an argument against a bubble, this interest rate story would have in fact implied a bubble. For more on this, see Baker (2002a).

32 The Census Bureau's vacancy data are available at
   http://www.census.gov/hhes/www/housing/hvs/hvs.html

The second phase of the housing bubble: 2002-2006

The housing bubble was already visible and large enough in 2002 that its collapse likely would have led to a recession in that year. However, rather than take any steps to rein in the bubble, the Federal Reserve Board and others in policy-making positions almost cheered it on. [33] Greenspan applauded subprime mortgages as a financial innovation that allowed moderate-income families who could not otherwise afford a home to buy one. [34] In early 2004, he even suggested that people could save money by taking out adjustable rate mortgages, in spite of the fact that the interest rate on 30-year fixed-rate mortgages was near a 50-year low. [35]

As tends to be the case in the later phases of bubbles, all the excesses of the early stages became ever more exaggerated. Weak lending standards became weaker. In its 2005 survey of homebuyers, the National Association of Realtors found that 43 percent of first-time homebuyers had made down payments of zero or less. [36] Banks were happy to make loans that were highly risky because they knew they could quickly sell them in the secondary market. In fact, many of the most aggressive subprime initiators, like Countrywide and Ameriquest, frequently filed inaccurate information for borrowers to allow them to get loans for which they were not qualified. Since they could sell these loans in the secondary market, they had little concern about the default risk. [37]

---

33 While higher interest rates will eventually deflate a bubble, the Fed was right to keep interest rates low at the time, given the weakness of the economy following the collapse of the stock bubble. The Fed has many other tools at its disposal, most immediately its ability to direct attention to a bubble. If the Fed had focused its research on documenting the evidence for a housing bubble, and Greenspan and other Fed officials had used congressional testimony and other public appearances to warn of the bubble, it is difficult to believe that they could not have curbed the irrational exuberance that was driving home prices higher. The Fed also has substantial regulatory power that it could have used to slow the tide of bad mortgages that was flooding the financial system.

34 Remarkably, Greenspan told the *Washington Post* that he had been unaware of the extent of the spread of subprime mortgages until January 2006, just as he was ending his tenure as Fed chairman (Klein and Goldfarb, 2008).

35 Kirchhoff and Hagenbaugh (2004).

36 Bishop, Hightower, and Bickicioglu (2005). Many people borrowed more than the purchase price of their homes, using the extra money to cover closing costs or other expenses.

37 See Hudson (2010).

The secondary market for subprime issuers was the major investment banks, which were eager to buy up as many mortgages as possible and resell them as mortgage-backed securities. These securities, as well as derivative instruments based on them, like collateralized debt obligations, could then be sold all over the world.

The investment banks cared little about the quality of the mortgages they stuffed into these securities, since they knew they could get an investment-grade rating on almost anything they put together. (The bond rating agencies are paid by the issuers, so the agencies had a major financial stake in keeping Goldman Sachs, Citigroup, and other major investment banks happy.) In this context, questionable mortgages and even outright fraud provided little reason for concern.

The federally chartered Federal National Mortgage Association and the Federal Home Loan Mortgage Corporation (Fannie Mae and Freddie Mac), identified as the main culprits in the housing debacle by many on the right, clearly contributed to the bubble by happily supplying mortgage credit throughout the run-up. Housing is their business, and they should have been able to recognize that prices had grown out of line with the fundamentals of the housing market. An explicit restriction on lending by one or both of these giants – for example, by basing loans on price-to-rent ratios instead of just appraised sale prices – likely would have been sufficient to deflate the bubble, especially if the agencies had aggressively argued their case in public. However, they followed along with everyone else.

But Fannie and Freddie were followers, not leaders. They were not the buyers of the worst subprime loans. This role fell to the major investment banks, which eagerly seized on a market that Fannie and Freddie had shunned. As a result, Fannie and Freddie's share of the secondary market plummeted in the years 2002-2005. They entered the subprime market in 2005, but did so to retake market share. As Moody's commented in a section labeled "Upcoming Challenges" in its 2006 assessment of Freddie:

> Freddie Mac has long played a central role (shared with Fannie Mae) in the secondary mortgage market. In recent years, both housing GSEs [government sponsored enterprises] have been losing share within the overall market due to the shifting nature of consumer

preferences towards adjustable-rate loans and other hybrid products. For the first half of 2006, Fannie Mae and Freddie Mac captured about 44 percent of total origination volume – up from a 41 percent share in 2005, but down from a 59 percent share in 2003. Moody's would be concerned if Freddie Mac's market share (i.e., mortgage portfolio plus securities as a percentage of conforming and non-conforming origination), which ranged between 18 and 23 percent between 1999 and the first half of 2006, declined below 15 percent. To buttress its market share, Freddie Mac has increased its purchases of private label securities. Moody's notes that these purchases contribute to profitability, affordable housing goals, and market share in the short-term, but offer minimal benefit from a franchise building perspective.[38]

In other words, Fannie and Freddie followed the investment banks into the subprime market, rather than led the way. And their reason for getting in was first and foremost the desire to maintain market share and increase profits, just like any other private business. The potential for extending homeownership to more moderate-income families was an afterthought added for public relations.

Remarkably, as the housing bubble was growing ever larger and the quality of mortgages continued to deteriorate, the government responded by loosening regulation. There had been several important moves toward deregulation in the Clinton years, most importantly the repeal of the Glass-Steagall Act, which allowed for the merger of investment banks and commercial banks, and the Commodities Futures Modernization Act, which restricted the regulation of derivatives. In the same vein, the Securities and Exchange Commission (SEC) in 2004 changed its rules on valuing assets (its "net capital rule") by allowing investment banks to value assets using their own modeling methods rather than standardized procedures. This change meant that these banks could conceal bad assets from scrutiny by regulators, as it appears Lehman was doing on a large scale at the time it went bankrupt.

It is not clear how much of a role the SEC's rule change played in the process, but the investment banks did become much more highly leveraged

---

38 Harris (2006) p. 6.

following it. They went from leverage ratios of less than 12-to-1 prior to the change to as high as 40-to-1 in the case of Bear Stearns at the time of its collapse.

2006: The end of the housing bubble
and the beginning of the collapse

Home prices peaked in the summer of 2006 and began to edge downward in the second half of the year. One widely used measure of home prices, the Case-Shiller 20 City index, was down by 3.5 percent from its summer peak by the end of 2006. It was inevitable that this decline would pick up steam. Once homebuyers no longer anticipated that prices would automatically rise every month, they became more cautious about buying.

The price declines created problems for lenders as well. As long as home prices keep rising, every loan is a good loan. If borrowers get in trouble they can always refinance based on the higher value of the home. Even if the borrower defaults, the bank gets possession of a property that is likely to be of greater value than the mortgage. All this changes once prices start falling. The subprime market began to freeze up in the second half of 2006, and by early 2007 it had become clear that there were major problems in the subprime market. It was in March 2007 that Fed Chairman Bernanke issued his famous comment that he expected the problems in the housing market to be contained to the subprime sector.[39]

The price decline accelerated over the course of 2007, with prices dropping by 2 percent in the first six months of the year and another 7 percent in the second half. By December 2007, when the recession officially began, prices had fallen by almost 11 percent from the peak of the bubble, implying a loss of more than $2.2 trillion in housing equity. With prices falling at the rate of 2 percent a month and the economy already shedding jobs due to the falloff in construction and weakening consumption as a result of lost wealth, it was inevitable that the bubble would continue to deflate.

At the point when the financial markets began to seize up in September 2008, home prices had fallen by almost 25 percent from their

---

39 Bernanke (2007).

bubble peaks, corresponding to a loss of more than $5 trillion in housing wealth. Given the extent of their losses and their extreme leverage, it was inevitable that major actors in the financial industry, including Fannie Mae and Freddie Mac, would take serious hits. The investment banks should not have been surprised since they had large amounts of mortgages, mortgage-backed securities, and derivative instruments that they had been unable to offload before the collapse of the market.

The financial crisis in the fall of 2008 undoubtedly sped up the pace of the downturn, and the economy went into a free fall until the spring of the next year. However, the economy's main problems – massive overbuilding in both the residential and nonresidential sectors, coupled with the prospect of losing $8 trillion in housing bubble wealth – were not the result of the financial crisis. These problems had pushed the economy into recession long before the financial crisis. It might have taken longer for their full effect to have been felt absent the crisis, but it is difficult to see any sector of the economy that would be stronger in the summer of 2011 than it is now had the financial crisis been averted. In short, this recession is the story of a collapsed housing bubble, not a financial crisis.

Chapter 5

Fulcrums of Power I:
The Fed and Interest Rates

The two most important levers of economic policy are the Federal Reserve Board, through its control of interest rates, and the Treasury, through its ability to influence the value of the dollar in international currency markets. Both policies are far removed from democratic control by explicit design, so it is difficult for even a well-informed public to alter them. However, it is essential that people at least understand how these levers are controlled so that they understand the ways in which government policy determines economic outcomes. We'll save the Treasury for Chapter 7 and focus on the Fed first.

The Fed's control of interest rates cannot always lift the economy quickly back toward full employment, since interest rates take a long time to affect the economy. And in an economy in which consumers are already heavily indebted and in no position to borrow more, as is the case in the United States in 2011, the Fed finds its traditional tools to be of relatively limited value.

But the Fed is not so hobbled when it wants to move the economy in the opposite direction. If it raises interest rates enough in response to real or imagined inflation, it will slow growth and reduce employment. Furthermore, if it has an unemployment target that it does not want to see breached — for example, a 6.0 percent estimate of the non-accelerating inflation rate of unemployment (NAIRU) — the Fed can raise interest rates enough to ensure that the unemployment rate does not fall below this level.

Who rules the Fed?

The Federal Reserve Board is further removed from democratic control than any other institution of the federal government, with the possible exception of the Supreme Court. Nothing symbolizes this lack of accountability better than the Fed's budget. In contrast to the Supreme Court, which must have its budget approved by Congress, the Fed draws up its own budget. The budget outlines the major streams of income flows (e.g., interest on holdings of government debt, fees from check clearing and foreign exchange clearing) and the major categories of spending. It simply sends over a copy of this budget to inform Congress, not to get congressional approval.

Under the law, the Fed is a mixed public-private entity. The public portion of the Fed, the board of governors, is located in Washington. The seven members of the board are appointed to 14-year terms by the president and approved by Congress. The length of the term is intended to give the governors considerable independence from the president who appointed them and the particular Congress that approved them. (As a practical matter, most governors do not serve full 14-year terms, and the average period of appointment is considerably shorter.) The chair of the board of governors is appointed to a 4-year term, although he or she can serve as a governor for 14 years. (By custom, chairs have resigned from the board at the end of their term as chair.)

The 12 district banks are the private portion of the Fed. Each of these banks is formally controlled by a nine-person board of directors. There are three categories of directors. The three Class A directors are selected by the banks in the district and are supposed to represent the interest of the banking industry. The three Class B directors are also selected by the banks in the district, but are supposed to represent other portions of the business community. The three Class C directors are selected by the board of governors in Washington and are supposed to represent broader segments of the community. Historically, Class C directors have included individuals associated with labor unions, consumer and community groups, and nonprofits, as well members of the business community.

This process for selecting directors basically puts the banks in control of the district Federal Reserve Banks. They appoint the Class A directors, who are by far the most important directors under the law. Furthermore, by virtue of their knowledge of banking, these directors are likely to be far more effective in influencing decisions than the Class B or Class C directors, who often have little background in finance or economics. While they may occasionally be able to raise a point for consideration by the board, it is highly unlikely that the Class B or Class C directors would be able to push an agenda item over the united opposition of the bank-appointed Class A directors.

Each district bank board picks a president. In addition to overseeing the operations of the district bank, the bank president also sits on the Federal Reserve Board's Open Market Committee (FOMC), which is the Fed's main decision-making body. The FOMC votes every six weeks on interest rate policy and monetary policy more generally. All seven governors are voting members of this committee, as is the president of the New York District Federal Reserve Bank, by far the most important district bank because its venue includes Wall Street. The other 11 bank presidents rotate into 4 remaining voting slots. This means that at any point in time, 5 of the 12 voting members of the FOMC will be individuals who were essentially selected by the banks. In addition, the seven other district bank presidents, who were also effectively appointed by the banks, take part in the policy discussion.

This formal structure creates a strong bias toward the interests of the banks in setting monetary policy, but the informal mechanisms pushing in this direction may be even stronger. The Fed was originally established in 1913 to provide a government backup for the banks. The immediate impetus was the financial crisis of 1907, in which the banker J.P. Morgan acted as a backstop to the financial system and helped to prevent a complete collapse. The country's leading bankers, recognizing the need to institutionalize the role played by Morgan in this crisis, lobbied Congress to establish the Fed.

The Fed's banker-friendly organizational structure was not an accident; it was first and foremost intended to serve the banks and only secondarily to serve the larger public. The Fed's culture is thoroughly intermeshed with the financial industry. While its legal mandate from Congress places an equal priority on the goals of price stability and full employment,[40] the Fed has maintained a much greater commitment to the former goal than the latter. In fact, current Fed Chairman Ben Bernanke has openly committed the Fed to targeting inflation at 2 percent, a policy which implies that the Fed would be willing to tolerate high jobless rates if it were concerned that more expansionary policy would raise the rate of inflation above its target.

Inflation is generally the main concern of the financial industry for the simple reason that its loans are fixed in dollar terms. If inflation reduces the value of the dollar, lenders lose money. This loss takes two forms. First, if inflation is running at a 5 percent annual rate, then the money paid back to lenders at the end of the year on loans they made at the beginning of the year is worth 5 percent less than the money they lent.

Of course if the banks had anticipated 5 percent inflation then they would adjust for this expectation in the interest rate they charge by adding into it this amount of expected inflation. If they were prepared to make a loan at 3 percent interest in a world with zero inflation, then they would demand 8 percent interest in a world where the inflation rate was expected to be 5 percent.

This brings up the second way in which banks lose money as a result of inflation. The bonds and loans they hold will fall in value in response to a rise in the rate of inflation. The price of bonds and long-term loans moves in the opposite direction of interest rates. If interest rates rise, then the price of these assets falls. And so if people come to expect higher rates of inflation, and then interest rates rise in response, the existing bonds and loans held by the banks will be worth less. For this reason, banks and other financial institutions typically face large losses if the rate of inflation increases.

This was the scenario that played out when many of the nation's savings and loan associations (S&Ls) became insolvent in the 1970s. S&Ls had issued low-interest mortgages in the low-inflation environment of the 1960s. When inflation reached double-digits in the late 1970s, the 30-year mortgages

---

40 The Federal Reserve Act, Section 2A, Monetary Policy Objectives, available at
    http://www.federalreserve.gov/aboutthefed/section2a.htm.

they had issued at 6 percent interest were suddenly worth much less. Since these mortgages were the primary asset of savings and loans (under the law, the vast majority of their lending had to be for residential housing), for many the losses on these mortgages exceeded their capital, making them insolvent.

It is not just the bank presidents who share the banks' concern about inflation. The governors of the Fed and most of its staff tend to share these concerns as well. They do not view the problem of high inflation and high unemployment as being symmetric.[41] The social circle in which these people circulate includes the top management of the country's largest banks, as well as their economists and other professional staff. It does not include union members, small business owners, or other actors in society who may have a different view on the tradeoffs between the risks of higher inflation and unemployment and slower growth. Any Fed governor committed to making lower unemployment the top priority, especially in a context where the policy risked higher rates of inflation, would face an enormous uphill struggle.

Another way to address this question of 'who rules the Fed' is by asking what sort of failures would get a Fed chairman fired. The last Fed chairman to be effectively fired was William Miller in the summer of 1979. He had been in the post for only 19 months. During this period, the rate of inflation had continued to accelerate, a process that had begun with the end of the recession in 1975, but the U.S. unemployment rate was just under 6 percent. Jimmy Carter replaced Miller with Paul Volcker, who was determined to bring down inflation regardless of the cost in unemployment. By January 1980, Volcker had raised interest rates enough to push the

---

41 On one occasion, a governor of the Fed acknowledged to me that there was little risk of runaway inflation even if the unemployment rate fell slightly below the so-called non-accelerating inflation rate of unemployment. He also acknowledged that there was little harm from moderate rates of inflation, meaning that if the Fed took this gamble and lost, there would be little cost associated with a rate of inflation that was stable, but slightly higher than the Fed's target. I asked why the Fed shouldn't take the virtually cost-free risk, and he responded by saying that the Fed is an institution that is committed to price stability. I pointed out that the Fed is also an institution that is committed to full employment, to which he replied that, "No one takes that commitment seriously." When I suggested that he then also doesn't need to take the commitment to price stability seriously, he responded, "Yes, I do."

economy into recession.[42] After a brief reprieve in the second half of 1980, he began to push up interest rates again. The economy returned to recession in July 1981, with unemployment peaking at just under 11 percent. Volcker was clearly serious about fighting inflation, and he retains a legacy as "a giant of the financial industry" who "restored credibility to the Federal Reserve."[43]

In a similar vein, Ben Bernanke was chairman of the Fed when the housing bubble collapsed and the banking crisis threatened to bring down the financial system. Even though the resulting fallout has given the country the worst downturn since the Great Depression, almost no one in a position of authority has suggested that Bernanke be fired for this policy failure.

While it is true that Bernanke only took over as Fed chair in January 2006, after the housing bubble had already expanded to a level where it would have been almost impossible to deflate without causing serious damage, Bernanke had been in top policy positions since the summer of 2002. He was a governor of the Fed until the summer of 2005, when he became the chief economist in the Bush administration. He remained there until he took over as Fed chair. During this time, he never raised any concerns about the housing bubble or the questionable finance that was fueling it. In fact, like Chairman Greenspan, he glibly dismissed anyone who raised questions along these lines.

In short, if the Fed's responsibility to maintain high levels of employment was taken seriously, it is difficult to imagine how someone could be more deserving of dismissal than Bernanke. The policy failures by Bernanke and his colleagues had disastrous consequences by this standard, yet neither he nor any of the other people in top positions at the Fed lost their jobs. In fact, their track record in leading the economy into disaster was never even raised seriously in policy debates.

We have to recognize that regardless of its legal mandate, as it stands now, the Fed is answerable to people who care much about inflation and little, if anything, about unemployment. Even modest increases in the rate of inflation are viewed as a high crime, despite the fact that there is little evidence that moderately higher inflation (e.g., 3 to 4 percent, as compared to 2

---

42 As a separate measure to slow consumption, Volcker also restricted the use of credit cards. At the time, the Fed had the ability to impose this type of credit control, but it does no longer.

43 *New York Times,* Times Topics.

percent) causes any serious harm to the economy. By contrast, even sharp divergences from full employment, which cause enormous suffering and massive losses of potential output, are not viewed as a serious failure by the interest groups to whom the Fed is accountable.

However bad the situation with the Fed, it is worth noting that it is likely the most democratic of the world's central banks, both in its levers of control and its mandate. Most other major central banks operate with a single mandate, to maintain price stability, which is generally specified as a 2 percent inflation target. These banks make no apology for the persistence of high rates of unemployment. It is officially not their job.

In terms of democratic accountability, it is possible to see how the Fed could be restructured to pursue policies that were more favorable toward the working population. In principle, Congress could strip the banks of their special power in determining the Fed's agenda by making all the Fed officials in decision-making positions presidential appointees subject to congressional approval. A president committed to appointing governors who focused on employment at least as much as price stability could change the Fed's orientation.

It is much more difficult to see how the European Central Bank (ECB) could be restructured to force it to serve the interests of Europe's workers rather than its financial sector. The European political structure is sufficiently convoluted that there is not even a clear mechanism to change an institution like the ECB: it was established to be in its current form indefinitely. A political movement hoping to alter this structure would be paving new ground altogether.

Regaining control over monetary policy

The Fed has been deliberately designed to insulate it from democratic control and leave it instead to be a tool of the financial industry. It will be hard to unrig the process, but there is no alternative to trying, given that the stakes for economic outcomes are so high. The long-term goal must be to establish the same sort of accountability from the Fed that would be expected from any other government agency. The Fed must answer to democratically elected officials.

However, any change in the governing structure of the Fed is many years in the future. In the meantime, we can take shorter-term steps to influence the Fed's behavior.

First, progressives can take a lesson from the right's message machine. After the initial phase of the financial crisis, many right-wing politicians and some economists began beating the drums about runaway inflation. Their argument was that the Fed's huge expansion of the money supply would inevitably cause prices to skyrocket. In reality, there was little reason to believe that inflation would be a problem at all. With massive amounts of idle capacity in almost every sector of the economy and an extraordinarily high unemployment rate, the conditions did not exist for inflation to take off. Furthermore, there had been prior instances in which central banks had vastly expanded a country's core money supply[44] during severe slumps, most obviously the Fed during the Great Depression and Japan's central bank in the 1990s. In both cases the money went to excess reserves, since banks faced no demand for loans in a depressed economy. Inflation did not result.

However unrealistic they may have been, the complaints by the right had their intended result. They bolstered the inflation hawks on the Fed and almost certainly made Chairman Bernanke and other relative doves more cautious about pushing expansionary monetary policy. In effect, those warning about inflation were able to get at least part of what they wanted: a Fed that was more cautious in stimulating the economy than would otherwise be the case.

How would the media, Congress, and the Fed have responded to an aggressive push in the opposite direction? Progressive members of Congress and other prominent political figures could have made a point of complaining that the Fed was taking inadequate steps to meet the portion of its mandate requiring it to pursue full employment.

Progressives could have called attention to the fact that Bernanke was not even following his own advice, offered while he was a professor at Princeton. In a 1999 paper harshly critical of the Japanese central bank's

---

44 The core money supply refers to the reserves that the Fed uses to buy government bonds, mortgage-backed securities, and other assets. These reserves are the basis for broader measures of the money supply.

response to that country's financial crisis, Bernanke argued that the Japanese bank should explicitly target a higher inflation rate in the range of 3 to 4 percent.[45] He argued that the higher rate would be desirable both because it would lower the real interest rate and also because it would reduce the debt burden of Japanese homeowners and corporations.[46]

Had a chorus arisen from the left that was remotely comparable to the absurd inflation fears raised by those on the right, it could have at least neutralized the pressure to tighten up on interest rates and slow economic growth. It's at least possible that such an effort could have paved the way for Bernanke to take more aggressive steps to boost the economy.

To illustrate the importance of the Fed to the economy, suppose that more aggressive monetary policy managed to boost growth by just 0.3 percent over the course of a year, certainly a modest target. A proportionate increase in employment would translate into 400,000 additional jobs. Job numbers of this size should be worth the attention of progressives. There have been major fights over policies that would have much less impact on employment.

Another aspect to the Fed's policy remarkably has received even less attention. When the Fed earns interest on the assets it holds, it refunds the money to the Treasury. In fiscal year 2010, the Fed paid the Treasury almost $80 billion as a result of the interest it earned on the government bonds and mortgage-backed securities it held.

Current budget projections assume that the Fed will sell off the assets it holds at present, so that the interest paid to the Treasury will diminish through time, even as interest rates rise when the economy recovers. But selling off these assets is a policy decision. The Fed could continue to hold its government bonds and refund the interest to the Treasury so that the interest does not pose as large a burden to the government in future years.

The potential impact of this decision is substantial. If the Fed held $3 trillion in government bonds over the next decade (roughly its current asset

---

45 Bernanke (1999).

46 The real interest rate is the nominal interest rate minus the inflation rate. The nominal interest rate cannot go below zero. Once the central bank has set the nominal interest rate at zero (as both the Japanese central bank did in the 1990s and the Fed has done in the Great Recession), the real interest rate cannot go lower unless the inflation rate rises.

level), it would reduce the interest burden to the government by a total of more than $600 billion.

Figure 5-1 shows the potential reduction in the national debt over the next decade as a result of a Fed policy to hold $3 trillion in assets compared to the impact of ending the Bush tax cuts on the richest 2 percent of the population.

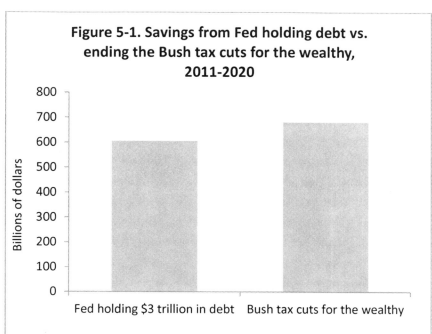

Figure 5-1. Savings from Fed holding debt vs. ending the Bush tax cuts for the wealthy, 2011-2020

Source: Fed holding debt: This calculation assumes that the Fed earns the same interest rate on $3 trillion in debt as the public on debt as a whole, with the interest rate calculated by taking the CBO projection of net interest divided by the prior year's debt; both are taken from CBO (2011a), Table 1-4. The projected interest rebated to the Fed (Table 4-2) is subtracted from this number. Bush tax cuts: Tax Policy Center (2010).

As can be seen, the potential impact on the debt of this virtually costless Fed policy is comparable to that of one of the policies that most dominates public debate. Yet, the idea of the Fed holding its assets to alleviate the interest burden of the debt is almost never discussed.[47]

If progressives were aware of the importance of the Fed in determining employment and other economic outcomes, they would almost certainly target more of their efforts on its policy decisions. The potential impact of the Fed on unemployment and wages dwarfs the impact of the vast majority of legislative items that garner attention from progressives. Even if the channels for directly changing Fed policy are limited, it is important for the public to understand the way in which Fed policy can hurt a person's ability to be employed and earn a decent wage.

This knowledge is also a necessary precondition for changing the structure of the Fed. As it stands now, most people have only the vaguest understanding of what the Fed is and very little idea of why it could be important in their lives. People recognize that the government can affect their well-being by raising or lowering taxes and cutting programs like Social Security and Medicare. There is almost no awareness that an agency of the government, the Federal Reserve Board, can pursue policies that will ensure that people remain employed or, alternatively, can maintain a sufficiently high rate of unemployment so that most workers will have little bargaining power with employers.

Opportunities suggest themselves for interesting and unusual coalitions in organizing to take on the Fed. Many grassroots libertarians are wary of the Fed, often because they view it as an instrument of Wall Street banks. Progressives can find allies among libertarians for at least some actions related to the Fed, most importantly measures that increase accountability.

In the last session of Congress, Ron Paul, one of its most conservative members, and Alan Grayson and Bernie Sanders, two of its most progressive, introduced bills requiring greater disclosure of the Fed's lending practices. Despite the opposition of the Democratic leadership, the Paul-Grayson bill

---

47 There is a concern that the bank reserves created by the Fed's holding assets could lead to inflation when the economy recovers. The Fed could head off inflation by raising bank reserve requirements, as an alternative to reducing the reserves of the banking system by selling assets. While this is a less-preferred tool of monetary policy, given the huge potential gains it is worth the risk. Scheduling the increases in advance could reduce any potential disruptions created by raising reserve requirements.

won the support of the majority of the House, as most Republicans and about one-third of Democrats signed on as co-sponsors. Despite the strong opposition of the Fed, which predicted disastrous consequences if details of loan information were made public, a version of these bills was eventually attached to the Dodd-Frank financial reform bill and passed into law. (To date, the disastrous consequences have not been apparent.)

Other measures like the Paul-Grayson-Sanders bills, that shine a spotlight on the Fed's actions, are likely to gain the support of a substantial number of libertarians. Many libertarians would prefer to shut down the Fed altogether, a move that would take away an important instrument for supporting the economy. [48] Though this goal will limit the degree of progressive cooperation with libertarians, on the issue of making the Fed more open and accountable, there is a clear common interest.

The long-term goal of Fed reform must be to strip the banking industry of its privileged role in determining Fed policy. The Fed should be restructured so that it operates in a similar manner to any other government agency, though even this change will not guarantee that it will act in the public interest. The Federal Communications Commission (FCC) is an independent agency answerable to Congress, but it would be hard to contest the fact that it often is more responsive to industry concerns than the interests of the general public. But at least Disney and Comcast do not get to directly appoint members of the FCC.

---

48 Rep. Paul wrote a book titled *End the Fed* so there is little ambiguity about the direction he would like to take.

Chapter 6

Full Employment without the Fed

In principle, the Fed should vigorously pursue policies that promote full employment.[49] However, it does not do so now, nor is it likely to do so in the near future. Under its current structure, the Fed is primarily responsive to the financial industry's concerns about inflation, and full employment comes in a distant second.

A progressive agenda should include efforts to educate the public about the Fed's importance and its structure, for two reasons: to maintain pressure on the Fed to pursue the full-employment portion of its mandate, and to create support for legally restructuring the institution so that it is more accountable to democratically elected officials.

But even in a best-case scenario, the Fed will be controlled by financial interests long into the future. This raises the question of whether there are other steps that can be taken to move the economy back toward full employment even when the Fed is at best indifferent – if not outright hostile – to this effort.

---

49 An earlier version of this chapter appeared as Baker (2011).

Work sharing: The quickest route back to full employment

In the absence of a growing demand for labor that would increase employment, an alternative route is to divide up the existing work among more workers. While this may be an inferior path — there is enormous waste associated with an economy operating below its potential — it may be the only route available given that the possibility of further fiscal stimulus appears to be blocked by political considerations. Yet, in any case, work sharing might be a proper route back to full employment, since there is nothing written in stone about the current length of the work week or work year.

Work sharing is not a new idea. The idea of shortening work time to create more jobs has a long history. In the context of an economy that is at full employment, the approach might be misguided, since legislated reductions in work time can lead to increased inflationary pressure and economic distortions. However, in an economy that is operating well below its potential and that is projected to remain below potential output for much of the next decade, as is the case with the U.S. economy, work sharing may be the most viable way of bringing the nation back to full employment.

Germany is the model in this respect. It has aggressively promoted a policy of work sharing, along with other measures aimed at persuading employers to retain workers. As a result, its unemployment rate stood at 6.1 percent in June 2011, 2.1 percentage points below the rate at the start of the downturn. [50] This remarkable achievement was not due to superior economic growth. Through the first quarter of 2011, the growth rate of Germany's economy since the start of the downturn had actually lagged somewhat behind the growth rate of the United States. The nearly steady fall in Germany's unemployment rate — at a time when the unemployment rate in the United States sharply increased and then remained high (peaking at 10.1 percent in October 2009 and only falling to 9.2 percent by June 2011), see **Figure 6-1** — was entirely due to different labor market responses to the downturn. [51]

---

50 This is the harmonized unemployment rate used by the Organization for Economic Cooperation and Development (OECD), which puts national rates on an internationally comparable basis.

51 See Schmitt (2011) for an analysis of the policy responses of the United States, Germany, and Denmark during this period.

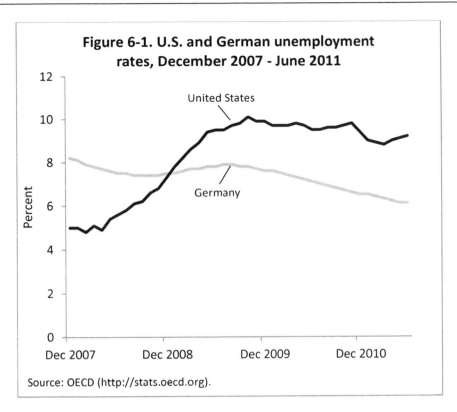

Figure 6-1. U.S. and German unemployment rates, December 2007 - June 2011

Source: OECD (http://stats.oecd.org).

Germany's experience with reducing work hours as an alternative to unemployment has been remarkable. But it is important to note that most of the reduction in work hours was not brought about by the formal short-work program run by the government. The OECD estimated that 25 percent of the reduction in hours worked in Germany resulted from the formal short-work program, 40 percent from employer agreements with unions or work councils, 20 percent from reduced overtime, and 20 percent from tapping work-hour accounts (accounts that allow workers to bank paid time off by working extra hours). [52] While the role of the short-work policy was important, it played out in the context of a larger commitment to preserving employment.

---

52 OECD (2010). When demand for labor fell in the recession, companies could cut back hours and maintain workers' pay by using hours in these accounts.

The overwhelming majority of the workers in short-work programs in Europe are men, disproportionately middle-aged, and tend to work for medium- and large-sized firms rather than smaller businesses. [53] The construction and manufacturing industries accounted for a hugely disproportionate share of participation in short-work programs, although they also accounted for the bulk of the job loss in the recession; hence, the concentration of covered workers in these sectors may be more a function of the pattern of job loss than the nature of the programs. By education level, workers with college and advanced degrees were underrepresented, as were workers without high school degrees. [54] The experience of short work in Europe suggests that it has primarily benefited a relatively narrow group of workers: less-educated middle-aged men in manufacturing and construction. To some extent this undoubtedly reflects features of the programs. For example, the programs generally place lower limits on the size of firms that can qualify. Insofar as men are more likely to be employed at larger firms, men will be overrepresented among the beneficiaries of the program. However, the fact that manufacturing and construction, which disproportionately employ men without college degrees, were hit hardest in the downturn also was important in determining the mix of beneficiaries from short-work programs.

The United States has limited experience with work sharing. States offering the programs tend to tie them to unemployment insurance: a worker receives unemployment benefits to make up for the income sacrificed for the shorter hours. Eighteen states had a work-sharing program attached to their unemployment insurance systems prior to the start of the recession, and several more states began the process of starting programs after the recession

---

53 This discussion relies largely on data from EFILWC (2010, Chapter 2).

54 An analysis of firms' participation in short-work programs in Germany by the International Labour Organization (Crimmann, Wießner, and Bellmann, 2010, p. 26) found a strong correlation between firm size and participation in work sharing programs. The use of freelancers was negatively correlated with participation, as was the percentage of college graduates among the workforce. Being involved in an export industry was highly correlated with participation, although this could also be attributable to the sharp drop in exports at the start of the downturn as opposed to the specific characteristics of these industries.

began.[55] Most of the existing programs date from the late 1970s or early 1980s. While some of the largest states, including California and New York, make work sharing available, the programs have had relatively little impact nationwide on unemployment in the downturn. Participation in work-sharing programs peaked in 2009 at just over 150,000 workers, less than 0.2 percent of payroll employment.[56] In only two states, Rhode Island and Kansas, did participation in work-sharing programs exceed 1.0 percent of payroll employment.

Since the end of 2009, participation in work-sharing programs has fallen sharply, due to the fact that participants in work sharing in most states are ineligible for extended unemployment benefits and in no state are they eligible for the Emergency Unemployment Compensation program that provides benefits for jobless spells lasting more than 52 weeks. This means that, for the most part, because participation in the program is tied to receipt of unemployment insurance benefits, workers can be on a work-sharing compensation program only for 26 weeks.

At the start of the downturn, layoffs occurred disproportionately in manufacturing and construction, the sectors where workers were most likely to take part in work-sharing programs. By the beginning of 2010, manufacturing had stopped shedding large numbers of jobs and the rate of job loss in construction had slowed sharply. As a result, the number of new entrants in work-sharing programs would have been expected to fall while many of the workers enrolled in the program would have reached the maximum length of time in which unemployment benefits compensated them for their reduced hours.

As it exists in the United States today, work sharing has at best had a marginal impact on employment, affecting only a small sliver of the workforce. The next section discusses some of the implementation issues that could make the program more attractive to both workers and employers.

---

55 President Obama's 2012 budget includes funding to support the establishment of work-sharing programs in states that do not already have them.
56 Email communication with Employment and Training Administration, U.S. Dept. of Labor, December 2010. See Woo (2011) for additional details.

Issues of implementation

Work-sharing programs in the United States are little changed from the time they were first put in place in the late 1970s and early 1980s. They tend to be overly bureaucratic and not well publicized. Many employers in the states where programs exist do not even know they might have the option to take advantage of them as an alternative to laying off workers.

One of the basic issues of implementation is the closeness with which employers are held to a specific plan for work sharing. Most states require that an employer certify that the proposed reduction in hours per worker is an alternative to layoffs, and it then must lay out a plan for reduced hours, usually for specific workers. This procedure allows individual workers to claim unemployment benefits against the scheduled reduction in work time. For example, if a worker is scheduled to have a reduction in work time of 20 percent, he or she can claim an unemployment insurance benefit equivalent to 20 percent of the benefit that would be available if the worker were unemployed altogether.[57]

This system has the disadvantage of both locking the employer into a specific pattern of hours reduction and requiring employees to individually apply for benefits. Drawing up a specific schedule of hours reduction and holding to it for a specified period may overly constrain employers operating in an environment where there is considerable uncertainty about demand for their products. The rigid scheduling can also be cumbersome, since any workplace will have some amount of turnover. If, for example, an employer moved a worker out of the work-sharing compensation system and into a full-time position elsewhere in the company, the firm could not replace the worker with another receiving work-sharing compensation without filing a new plan with the state employment agency.

These restrictions can be avoided if the employer is given more discretion over which workers are covered and how much work time is actually reduced. In this case, the state agency would probably make payments directly to the company rather than to the individual worker. The payments could be made based on scheduled reductions in hours and then adjusted in

---

57 This discussion follows that of Messenger (2009).

accordance with the actual reduction in hours on a quarterly or annual basis. While this system would leave more opportunities for abuse, the experience rating of insurance payments[58] should limit the extent to which employers have incentive to game the system. An employer that deliberately flouted the system would find itself faced with much higher payments into the system in subsequent years.[59]

Two other important issues of implementation affect the willingness of workers to accept work sharing. First, there is the question of whether fringe benefits are still paid for the workers for the hours they are not working. The state programs are based on wage compensation, so in many cases workers seeing a 20 percent reduction in work hours will also see a 20 percent reduction in the portion of health insurance premiums paid by their employer as well as a 20 percent reduction in contributions to pensions or other benefits. This reduction in benefits could be a substantial disincentive to workers to take part in a work-sharing program.

The other issue is that work-sharing benefits generally count against regular unemployment benefits. If a worker has been in a work-sharing program for, say, 20 weeks with hours reduced by 20 percent, then upon being laid off the duration of work-sharing would reduce the eligibility period for conventional unemployment insurance by 4 weeks. Since firms that use work-sharing are experiencing shortfalls in demand almost by definition, there is a high probability that there will be layoffs at some point. The concern over the possibility of being laid off with a reduced period of eligibility for benefits could make workers reluctant to take part in work-sharing programs.

---

58 Experience rating is the comparison of the insured's actual loss against losses common to similar workers, or in this case, the work-sharing experience of a given firm compared to similar firms.

59 This situation involves two potential risks. The first is that a firm in a shaky position financially may opt to abuse the system, recognizing the likelihood that it will not survive long enough to ever repay more than a fraction of the excess benefits claimed, or that new firms may not stay in business long in any case. To limit this avenue of abuse, if a firm did not appear to be financially stable, then the state employment agency could be given the option to refuse a work-sharing plan on this basis. The other opportunity for abuse would be if employers claimed the benefit without actually reducing workers' hours. There could also be a requirement that employers post any approved work-sharing plans in a visible place at their workplace so that workers could easily find them and verify that they were actually seeing the reductions in work hours claimed by their employers.

There is also the problem noted earlier that workers in work-sharing programs generally are not eligible for benefits beyond an initial 26-week period. This means that only those experiencing relatively short spells of reduced work hours will be able to take part in work-sharing programs.

All of these problems can be addressed in ways that are likely to increase the use of work-sharing with only a modest commitment of additional resources to the program. All else equal, when it comes to reducing their demand for labor, employers should be largely indifferent to whether it's by laying off workers or reducing hours for the existing workforce.[60] Since there is a clear public interest in keeping people employed, it would make sense to structure a work-sharing program in ways that make it more desirable than laying off workers from the standpoint of employers, even if it comes at a somewhat higher cost to the government than the current unemployment insurance system.

Specifically, it could be desirable to pay a premium of 25 to 30 percent to companies in excess of what their workers would receive in unemployment insurance benefits if a comparable reduction in work hours had to be accomplished through layoffs. This system would best take the form of an employer credit,[61] so that workers would not have to individually file for the benefit and employers would have the freedom to alter work weeks as needed and change the specific workers who were receiving work-sharing compensation. The program could require that employers maintain their full contributions for health insurance, defined-benefit pensions, and any other benefits that are not easily divisible. The increased premium could also be used to cover an additional period of eligibility for conventional unemployment insurance if workers on work-sharing programs were laid off. This enhanced protection should make workers more willing to accept work-sharing plans.

---

60 Employers are likely to prefer work sharing to layoffs in many cases since it means that they can retain skilled workers. When demand increases they just have to raise workers' hours rather than find and train new workers.

61 See Baker (2009b).

The impact of work sharing on employment

There is evidence available for predicting the take-up rates for a more generous work-sharing program. With other policies, like wage subsidies, it is possible to derive a projected impact based on estimates of the elasticity of labor demand (i.e., the extent to which lowering the cost of labor leads firms to add workers). In the case of work sharing, demand is not really an issue since the immediate goal is not to increase the demand for labor but rather to change its distribution. The relevant question is the willingness of employers to take part in the program and to readjust patterns of work to meet its requirements. The answer will depend both on the extent to which employers view the program as advantageous to keep workers on the payroll and on the costs of making the necessary adjustments in the structure of work.

Based on the German experience, it is possible that employers will view shortening work hours as preferable to layoffs, even with little or no additional subsidy from the government. German employers have been supportive of the country's short-work policy in large part because they recognize the advantage of having workers on their payrolls whose hours can be increased quickly when demand grows, as opposed to the disadvantage of spending time and money hiring new workers. However, there are other features of Germany's labor market, which do not exist in the United States, that make short work relatively more attractive there.

First and foremost, Germany has a far higher union coverage rate, with approximately 43 percent of its workers covered by collective bargaining agreements compared to about 13 percent in the United States.[62] This means that German employers are more likely to have to negotiate layoffs with a union rather than unilaterally lay off workers. Second, firms with more than 250 employees are required to have a works council, which would play a role in any layoff decisions. In addition, employment protection rules in Germany do not allow employers to dismiss most workers at will. Thus, German employers have a strong incentive to develop plans for reducing work hours in ways that are acceptable to their workers.

---

62 See Visser (2011). The U.S. figure here is Visser's "adjusted coverage." The German figure is Visser's unadjusted coverage; the adjusted figure for Germany is 63 percent.

At the same time, employers in the United States do recognize the benefits of keeping their incumbent workers on the job rather than being forced to hire new workers when demand increases. In the latest downturn the length of the average workweek fell substantially in every sector of the economy, an indication that employers did not adjust labor demand exclusively through layoffs. If a better advertised, more generous, and less bureaucratic system were in place, surely employers would be more likely to take advantage of the option of work-sharing.

A relatively simple calculation can tell us with some certainty the cost per job, if not the number of jobs saved. If the target is to increase the generosity of the unemployment insurance system by 30 percent by having the system cover non-wage benefits for workers on work-sharing and implicitly by extending the length of unemployment benefits through not counting the period of work-sharing against the benefit limits, then the cost per job saved would be roughly 30 percent of the average unemployment benefit. With benefits currently averaging $300 a week or $15,000 a year, a more generous system of work-sharing would cost roughly $4,500 per job saved.

Table 6-1 shows the impact of this policy on employment by industry assuming take-up rates by employers for job losses of 10 percent, 15 percent, and 20 percent. In other words, 10 percent, 15 percent, and 20 percent of the workers who would otherwise be dismissed are instead kept on as a result of work-sharing programs. The numbers showing the projected impact at the end of the year assume that the average period that workers are in a work-sharing program is six months. An average hours reduction of 20 percent would imply that the total number of workers in work-sharing programs is five times as large as the number of jobs saved.

Table 6-1
Potential impact of work sharing on employment, thousands

	Average monthly rate of layoffs or discharge, 2010	Take-up rate (impact on employment at year end)		
		10%	15%	20%
Government	124	74.2	111.3	148.4
Total private	1594	956.5	1434.8	1913.0
Mining	15	9.0	13.5	18.0
Construction	262	157.2	235.8	314.4
Manufacturing	137	82.2	123.3	164.4
Wholesale Trade	59	35.4	53.1	70.8
Retail Trade	190	114.0	171.0	228.0
Transportation	53	31.8	47.7	63.6
Information	23	13.8	20.7	27.6
Finance and Insurance	35	21.0	31.5	42.0
Real Estate	25	15.0	22.5	30.0
Prof. & Bus. Services	343	205.8	308.7	411.6
Education and Health	169	101.4	152.1	202.8
Leisure and Hospitality	222	133.2	199.8	266.4
Other services	72	43.2	64.8	86.4
Total	**1718**	**1030.7**	**1546.1**	**2061.4**

Source: Bureau of Labor Statistics, Job Openings and Labor Turnover Survey.
(Calculations assume that workers stay on work-sharing an average of six

If these targets are plausible, then the potential of work sharing on employment is substantial. A 10 percent take-up rate from a more flexible work-sharing program would increase employment by more than one million. With a 20 percent take-up rate, employment would rise by more than two million. Based on the pattern of layoffs by industry, the biggest impact would be in the professional and business service sector.[63] The next largest impacts would be in construction and the leisure and hospitality sector.

Two important factors are likely to cause the take-up rate by industry to be different from the rate of job loss by industry: firm size and pay rates. As noted before, smaller firms are generally prohibited from participating in work-sharing programs. The rationale for excluding smaller firms is that it

---

63 This may be somewhat misleading, since business and professional services includes the temporary employment sector.

would be difficult to monitor their compliance, and it would be more difficult for them to reorganize their workplaces to adjust to shorter workweeks.

Table 6-2 shows the percentage of job loss in the first two quarters of 2010 by firm size. Most of the job loss occurred in smaller firms during this period, with firms with more than 50 employees accounting for just 35.8 percent of the gross job loss. This means that if eligibility for participation were restricted to firms that employ more than 50 workers, then the take-up rate among eligible firms would have to be almost three times the levels shown in Table 6-1 in order to reach the same employment growth targets. Achieving a 10 percent take-up rate among all workers who would otherwise lose their jobs would require a take-up rate of almost 28 percent among firms that employed more than 50 workers; an overall 20 percent take-up rate would require a take-up rate of almost 56 percent among firms employing more than 50 workers. If the cutoff for participation were instead put at 20 employees, then there would have to be a 21 percent take-up rate among the eligible firms to reach the 10 percent target and a 42 percent rate to reach the 20 percent target.

Table 6-2
Share of job loss by firm size, 2010 (quarters 1 and 2)

Firm Size	Share of job loss
1-4	14.3
5-9	10.3
10-19	10.2
20-49	11.5
50-99	6.9
100-249	7.1
250-500	4.2
500-999	3.5
Over 1000	14.2
More than 20 workers	47.3
More than 50 workers	35.8

Source: Bureau of Labor Statistics, Business Employment Dynamics.

Finally, the take-up rate is likely to be affected by pay levels. Since unemployment benefits are capped in most states at relatively low levels, the potential compensation provided through a work-sharing program will be a smaller share of the wages of highly paid employees than of relatively low-paid workers. **Table 6-3** shows data from the Current Population Survey on the distribution of hourly wages by industry for 2010. By wage distribution, the retail sector, restaurants, and hotels would seem to have the largest proportion of workers who could benefit from a work-sharing program. Of course, these sectors also have many small employers that would likely not be eligible, and so the highest take-up rate could be expected to be among the larger establishments.

Table 6-3
Industries of workers, by hourly wage quintile, 2010

	10th	25th	50th	75th	90th
Computer and electronic products	11.1	16.8	26.2	38.5	59.8
Professional and technical services	12.0	17.0	25.6	38.5	57.4
Telecommunications	11.1	15.9	23.5	33.8	48.1
Transportation equipment manuf.	11.0	15.4	23.0	34.0	47.5
Hospitals	10.5	14.3	21.9	32.1	44.4
Finance	10.5	14.0	21.0	34.1	56.6
Wholesale trade	9.6	12.7	18.3	26.4	40.0
Construction	10.0	12.5	18.0	26.0	37.0
Real estate	9.0	12.0	17.0	25.0	38.9
Health care services, except hospitals	8.7	10.8	15.5	24.0	37.4
Arts, entertainment, and recreation	7.8	9.5	13.6	20.0	30.5
Administrative and support services	8.0	9.5	12.5	19.2	29.6
Retail trade	7.8	9.0	12.0	18.0	26.7
Accommodation	7.5	9.0	12.0	16.8	24.6
Food services and drinking places	7.3	8.0	9.6	13.1	19.2

Source: Analysis of CEPR extract of Current Population Survey Outgoing Rotation Survey (CPS ORG), 2010.

The longer-term benefits of work sharing

Work sharing offers the short-term benefit of allowing a return to something resembling full employment in a reasonable period. However, its potential long-term benefits could be at least as important. In 1980, the average number of hours worked by full-time workers in the United States was not very different than in other wealthy countries. But in the decades since 1980 most other wealthy countries have seen sharp reductions in work hours in favor of paid vacation days, paid family leave, and paid sick days. In many countries, the standard workweek is now considerably less than 40 hours. As a result, the typical full-time worker in Western Europe puts in many fewer hours than the typical worker in the United States; in some countries the gap in hours for full-time workers is more than 20 percent. **Figure 6-2** illustrates the U.S. place in the industrialized world in terms of paid parental leave, and **Figure 6-3** shows where it falls in legislated vacation time.

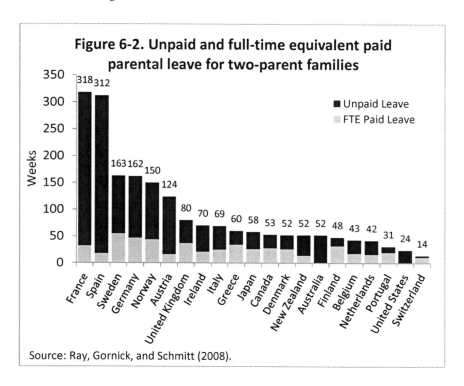

Figure 6-2. Unpaid and full-time equivalent paid parental leave for two-parent families

Source: Ray, Gornick, and Schmitt (2008).

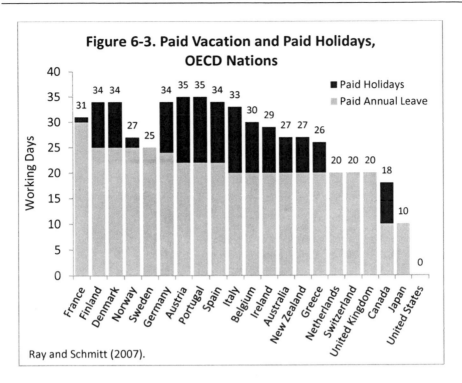

Figure 6-3. Paid Vacation and Paid Holidays, OECD Nations

Ray and Schmitt (2007).

There are reasons to think it would be a good thing for the United States to follow the path of Western Europe in having shorter work weeks. The move to shorter work weeks in many cases was intended to ensure more family-friendly workplaces. Paid family leave means that workers in Western Europe can stay home to care for young children or elderly parents. Paid sick days mean that a parent doesn't have to worry about losing his or her job to care for a sick child. And paid vacation time means that workers are guaranteed some time off that they can spend with family and friends. These are all benefits that can be viewed as substantially increasing the quality of life.

Of course there is a tradeoff. The cost of working fewer hours is that per capita income in Western Europe averages more than 20 percent less than in the United States. There is little difference in productivity – output per hour – between Western Europe and the United States, and in effect workers in Europe have taken much of the benefits of productivity growth over the last three decades in leisure rather than income. (It is worth noting that the gap in incomes between the United States and Western Europe refers to average incomes. The gap at the median, if it exists at all, is considerably smaller.)

While Europeans no doubt appreciate the greater amount of leisure that they enjoy compared with their counterparts in the United States, it is not obvious that they suffer as a result of a lower average income. There is undoubtedly a substantial relative component in assessments of well-being, so if a job in Germany or Belgium pays a wage that is close to the median, it is likely that workers feel reasonably contented with their standard of living even if it leaves them with a somewhat lower material standard of living than a similar U.S. worker. Not being able to afford a new car every few years may be less of a concern if people buy new cars rarely compared with a country where workers buy new cars more frequently.

Another aspect of the labor-leisure trade-off is that there is a strong correlation between greenhouse gas emissions and income. [64] Essentially, wealthier people use more energy and therefore have more greenhouse gas emissions. Western Europe emits approximately half as much greenhouse gases per capita as the United States. [65] There are two obvious explanations for this gap. First, because people in the United States have more money, they are more able to afford items such as big cars or the cost of air conditioning their homes to very low temperatures in the summer. And if Europeans have more time, they may place less of a premium on driving their own cars, as opposed to taking public transportation or riding a bicycle, to get somewhere a few minutes faster. Because time is at much more of premium in the United States, people are willing to pay a higher price in terms of money and energy to save time.

Thus, in addition to the benefits of making work more family friendly and improving the quality of life, there are also environmental reasons for preferring that people take the benefits of productivity growth in the form of more leisure rather than income. Yet to date, environmentalists have not taken much notice of the potential to reduce greenhouse gas emissions and other pollutants by promoting shorter work weeks or work years.

When considering measures that are designed to influence the length of the work week or work year, it is important to remember that it was not just the market that determined the work schedules we have today. One of the

---

64   Rosnick and Weisbrot (2006).
65   United Nations Statistics Division (2010).

main reasons employers are reluctant to add more workers and reduce the hours of the current workforce is the overhead cost of hiring a worker, most importantly health care costs. Typically health care is a per-worker expense: employers pay a fixed amount for a worker's health insurance policy regardless of how many hours he or she actually works.[66]

The structure of health care provision in the United States was not determined by accident. It dates back to World War II, when employer-provided health insurance became a mechanism for raising compensation while evading wartime wage-price controls. Also, the policy of exempting employer-provided insurance from the income tax (along with most other employer-provided benefits) gave firms an incentive to provide a substantial portion of workers' compensation in health care and other non-wage benefits.

This history is relevant because it means that the current length of the average work year is not simply the result of the workings of the market and the preferences of employers and employees. Government policy provided substantial incentives for hiring fewer workers for more hours rather than more workers for shorter hours. Since policy got us here, there is no reason to be shy about using policy to set the economy on a different course.[67]

Work sharing as a state-based way to get to full employment

One of the best things about work sharing is that it can be implemented largely at the state level, especially if the federal government provides some leeway in restructuring unemployment insurance. States could experiment with different structures to see which is most successful in maximizing take-up by employers and minimizing fraud.

---

66 Firms often a have a category of workers they define as "part time" who work less than 35 or 30 hours a week and therefore are not given health care, whereas full-time employees receive insurance. It is becoming more common for employers to pay a certain amount toward a worker's insurance policy (rather than paying for the policy itself). In some cases this sum would be paid on a per-hour basis, but this is more the exception than the rule. The vast majority of health care policies are still paid for as a fixed amount per worker.

67 It is worth noting that the higher marginal tax rates in European countries relative to the United States provide a greater incentive in these countries to take the benefits of productivity growth in leisure. If workers took the benefits in higher pay, they would see less gain after-tax than their counterparts in the United States.

While the political establishment in the United States is very effective at ignoring policy successes in other countries (how often have you heard about Germany's 6.1 percent unemployment rate?), it is more difficult to ignore successes at the state level. If Ohio or Washington State implemented a work-sharing program that pushed their unemployment rates under 5.0 percent, they would provide a model that other states would want to emulate. So even if gridlock at the national level prevents any major work-sharing initiative, there is nothing to prevent innovative action at the state level.

A successful work-sharing initiative can accomplish several goals simultaneously. First and most importantly, it will keep people at work, a hugely important objective in a context of high national unemployment. As people are out of work for longer periods, it becomes increasingly difficult for them to find re-employment. Many of the long-term unemployed may never find work again. The devastation to individual workers and their families from this situation is enormous, as is the waste to the economy when qualified and willing workers are unable to find jobs. If work sharing can substantially reduce the number of unemployed, it will be a beneficial policy in both the short and long term.

Work sharing can be coupled with policies that make the workplace more family friendly. These include paid family leave, sick days, and paid vacation. The United States lags far behind other wealthy countries in providing these benefits to its workers. Incentives for shortening the work week or work year as opposed to laying off workers should help to offset the institutional factors that have led employers to prefer longer hours to the hiring of additional workers.

Furthermore, work sharing can be coupled with environmental benefits. Structuring incentives to encourage workers to take the gains of productivity growth partly in leisure rather than income would almost certainly lead to a reduction in greenhouse gas emissions. For example, if participants in a work-sharing program were to work four, instead of five, days per week, that would mean one less day per week per worker of the pollution associated with commuting.

As a final note, it is worth thinking about the labor market dynamics of promoting a reduction in hours through a system of work sharing as opposed to layoffs through unemployment insurance. The system of work sharing is most likely to primarily affect the less-educated portion of the labor force, both because less-educated workers are more likely to face unemployment, and because unemployment insurance benefits are capped, meaning that the program would pay a larger share of the wage package of a less-educated workers than that of more highly educated workers.

A reduction in the typical work year for less-educated workers would have the same effect on the labor market for these workers as a reduction in their supply, and reducing their supply would be expected to increase their bargaining power and their relative wages. In other words, if institutional changes led to a reduction in standard work years by 20 percent, this would have the same effect on the labor market as reducing the supply of workers by 20 percent. It is basic economics that wages are to a large extent determined by supply and demand. Most economists attribute the rise in wage inequality over the last three decades to the fact that the increase in the supply of less-educated workers has exceeded the increase in the demand for them. However, policies that have the effect of reducing the average number of hours worked would put upward pressure on the wages of less-educated workers in the same way as a reduction in the number of workers or an increase in the demand for their work. In other words, work-sharing is a policy that would structure the market in a way that reduces inequality.

Chapter 7

Fulcrums of Power II:
The Treasury and the Dollar

The U.S. Treasury's ability to influence the value of the dollar in international currency markets might at first seem to be a trivial power that matters little to ordinary people, unless they travel abroad or happen to be employed in an import-export business. But it is a power that can and does have a major impact, not only on the unemployment rate but also on which workers become unemployed and how much employed workers earn. And it is a power exercised with little understanding or oversight by the public.

The Treasury has the authority to intervene directly in currency markets by buying or selling dollars, though it rarely uses this authority. (The Treasury can in principle coordinate its interventions with the Fed, which also holds a large amount of foreign currency.) Usually its efforts to influence the value of the dollar have been more subtle, such as making pronouncements about a "strong dollar," or indirect, through its control of the International Monetary Fund.

Nonetheless, the Treasury could intervene more actively in currency markets if it opted to do so. Acting in coordination with the Fed, the Treasury could choose to bring the value of the dollar down against other currencies, and thereby produce a huge improvement in the country's trade balance. In turn, this would create millions of new manufacturing jobs. A boost to manufacturing would increase the demand for non-college-educated workers and push up their wages relative to those of more highly educated workers. There is remarkably little awareness, even in policy circles, that the value of the dollar is a policy tool under the control of the government. This is striking because there have been major debates over trade agreements like NAFTA and CAFTA (The Central American Free Trade Agreement), primarily over concern about their potential impact on jobs in the United States. By contrast, the value of the dollar is almost never mentioned in policy debates. Even small changes in the value of the dollar are likely to have far more impact on trade and employment than the most important of these trade agreements. Typically, trade pacts comprise relatively small reductions in tariff barriers, coupled with changes in investment rules designed to facilitate the movement of manufacturing jobs overseas. Even the largest of the recent trade pacts involved only a relatively small portion of U.S. trade – for example, the entry of Mexico into NAFTA.

A rise in the value of the dollar against other currencies by, say, 10 percent is equivalent to giving a 10 percent subsidy on all the goods imported into the United States and imposing a 10 percent tariff on all the goods we export. This sort of increase in the value of the dollar could easily increase the trade deficit by more than 1 percent of GDP (about $150 billion), an amount that would imply the loss of far more than one million jobs. Yet, such an increase in the value of the dollar could occur over a couple of months and get almost no mention outside of the business pages, and even then would not likely garner major headlines.

This works to the advantage of those who benefit from a high-dollar policy. At the top of this list would be the financial industry, which receives benefits of a high dollar through two channels. First, by making imports cheaper, a high dollar helps to keep inflation low, and stable prices are a financial industry obsession. Second, when the financial industry looks to move abroad, its dollar assets go much further when the dollar is overvalued.

Other industries have a more ambiguous view toward a high dollar. Domestic manufacturers should oppose a high dollar since it places them at a disadvantage relative to their foreign competitors. However, insofar as manufacturers are able to establish operations overseas, they are likely to be content with a high-dollar policy that disadvantages only some of their operations. Because they can shield themselves with their foreign operations, they can gain an advantage over purely domestic competitors.

Major retail chains like Wal-Mart are advantaged in a similar way. By contracting with suppliers in China and other countries with low labor costs, these chains enjoy a supply of low-cost imports that allows them to undercut retailers that pay higher domestic prices for their products. For this reason, major retailers are likely to oppose any effort to lower the value of the dollar.

There is also a peculiar class dynamic to the dollar debate. When American tourists travel to Europe or Asia, their money goes further when the dollar is high. While only a small portion of the population makes regular trips overseas, it is an important group for policy purposes. The people who staff congressional offices and the higher levels of the bureaucracies in Washington, the people who run and contribute to political campaigns, and the reporters who cover them all are likely to be among the group of frequent foreign travelers. For all these people, a decline in the dollar might be viewed as bad news because it means that their next trip to France or Italy will cost more.

The importance of this aspect of the policy debate should not be underestimated. Even the staffers of progressive members of Congress and journalists from progressive opinion magazines are far more likely to take vacations in Europe than the typical person. It is easy for them to understand that a high dollar makes their overseas trips less expensive. This fact can make it much harder for them to understand that a high dollar can also cause millions of workers to be unemployed or force them to work at lower wages.

While a substantial number of powerful special interest groups will benefit from an overvalued dollar, it is harmful to the economy as a whole in both the short run and the long run. In the short run, an overvalued dollar virtually guarantees a large trade deficit, and a trade deficit both reduces overall employment and changes the mix of jobs in a way that works against workers without college degrees. The jobs that are lost as a result of a trade deficit will be disproportionately in manufacturing, which continues to be a source of relatively high-paying jobs for less-educated workers. For this reason, the trade deficit is an important factor contributing to the increase in inequality that we have seen over the last three decades.

It is also important to recognize how the dynamics of a trade deficit affect the overall economy. If the country has a trade deficit, then it is, on net, borrowing from abroad. In other words, someone must be lending us money in some form to allow us to buy more than we are selling. If the country as a whole is borrowing more than it is lending, then the culprit must be either the public sector or the private sector. (That's all we've got.)

Borrowing on the public-sector side corresponds to the large budget deficits that we hear so much about. A budget deficit means that the government is spending more than it pulls in as tax revenue and therefore must borrow the difference. A large budget deficit can be one result of a large trade deficit. The causation would be that the loss of jobs due to the trade deficit reduces tax revenues and increases payouts for unemployment insurance and other benefits. In this story, if we get the dollar down, then we can make substantial progress in reducing the budget deficit, since the jobs created by reducing the trade deficit will lead to more income tax revenue and lower benefit payments.[68]

If the budget is near balance or in surplus, then the borrowing must be on the private side. This would be the story of extraordinarily low private savings that we saw during the years of both the stock and housing bubbles. In both cases, the inflow of foreign capital helped to inflate the bubbles. The wealth created by these bubbles led people in the United States to spend more and save less, yielding large negative private savings. This is not a sustainable course, since bubbles eventually burst.

Recovering from a burst asset bubble can be a long and difficult process, as the country is now experiencing. If the dollar does not fall enough

---

68 Deficit hawks generally reverse this chain of causation, claiming that the budget deficit is responsible for the trade deficit. This can be true if the budget deficit leads to higher interest rates, which in turn raise the value of the dollar, as investors want to buy dollar assets to take advantage of high U.S. interest rates. No one ever opts to buy an imported product instead of a domestically produced item because of the budget deficit. They choose to buy the imported product because it is cheaper. However, if the dollar stays high, then reducing the budget deficit will not affect trade — unless it leads to a decline in GDP and employment. In short, if the goal is to reduce the trade deficit by reducing the budget deficit, then the intention must be to lower the value of the dollar or raise the unemployment rate. Anyone who wants to combine a low budget deficit and a high dollar, and still have a low trade deficit, wants a high unemployment rate. There is no plausible way to avoid this conclusion.

to allow the trade deficit to get much closer to balance, then the government must run large budget deficits to sustain employment. The only alternative would be to create yet another bubble to drive the economy.

A high trade deficit means that we have either a large budget deficit and/or low private savings. This is what in economics and finance is called an accounting identity: there is no way around this fact.

Getting the dollar under control

The story with the dollar is similar to the story with the Fed. As with the Fed, there is little ability for the public to directly influence a policy that is set by the Treasury with no obvious mechanisms for congressional input. However, the Treasury is susceptible to public pressure, just like any other government agency.

The first step must be to raise awareness of the importance of the dollar in determining the trade balance and therefore both the number and mix of jobs in the economy. Although the topic is taught in every introductory economics class, few people in Washington policy debates understand the basics of the relationship between the value of the dollar and the trade balance. For this reason, the issue is, at best, part of a larger laundry list of concerns to be raised in the context of trade. Few recognize that lowering the value of the dollar will almost certainly have more impact than all the other items on the list put together.

In addition to understanding the economic impact of an overvalued dollar, the public should also recognize how interests divide on this issue. It is standard practice for politicians to treat dollar policy as something outside of the control of the U.S. government. Consider, for example, what we have read about the need for the U.S. to confront China over its currency "manipulation," that is, its practice of deliberately depressing the value of its currency against the dollar.

There are several aspects of this framing of the issue that are inaccurate. First, China has an explicit policy of pegging its currency to the dollar. This is not something it is doing in the dark when no one is looking, so the use of the term "manipulation" is not really appropriate. It is also worth noting that China is hardly the only country that pegs its currency to the dollar; many other developing countries do so as well. However, China is by far the biggest, and the others are likely to let their currencies follow the Chinese currency upward against the dollar.

Second, when the United States discusses currency values with China, it is in the context of a range of economic and non-economic issues. Because China is a great power, it does not just agree to whatever the United States demands from it. It makes concessions on some issues in exchange for concessions on other issues from the United States.

When U.S. negotiators confront China with their list of issues, one of which includes raising the value of the renminbi (RMB) against the dollar, they are not likely to get concessions on the RMB unless it is clearly identified as a top priority issue – one for which the United States is prepared to make concessions on other issues. If the U.S. negotiators do not bring out the currency issue front and center, then the Chinese will understand that the U.S. government is not especially concerned about it.

In fact, the Chinese would likely reach the conclusion that the U.S. negotiators were just raising the currency issue for show; our negotiators could honestly claim that they had pressed the Chinese government to raise the value of its currency, but the Chinese refused to yield. This sort of charade has allowed both the Obama and Bush administrations to claim that they are concerned about the overvaluation of the dollar and that they are doing what they can to rectify the situation.

Yet the United States has the power to unilaterally take steps to lower the value of the dollar against other currencies. It can be difficult or even impossible to keep the price of a currency above the market-clearing level, but it is always possible to push down the value of a currency, through relatively simple mechanisms.

One route, which is completely legal under all U.S. trade agreements, would be to tax the interest earnings of a country that we believe is maintaining an undervalued currency against the dollar. For example, the United States could impose a 20 percent tax on all of the earnings on dollar assets held by China's central bank or state-owned enterprises. It could then raise the tax by 10 percentage points a year if China refused to reduce its dollar holdings and allow the value of its currency to rise.[69] This would eventually impose a sizable penalty on the Chinese government, making its high-dollar policy ever more costly.

The U.S. government has other, more extreme options available to force down the value of the dollar against the RMB. One would be to simply establish an exchange rate that set a much higher price for the RMB. For example, the U.S. could set a price of 4 RMB to the dollar instead of the rate of close to 6.6 RMB to the dollar set by the Chinese government. While it would be illegal, under Chinese law, for Chinese companies or citizens to sell currency to the Treasury at this U.S.-set rate, given the enormous potential gains, it is likely that many Chinese companies and wealthy individuals would find ways to evade the law. This could have the effect of making the U.S. Treasury rate the effective exchange rate in the rest of the world.[70]

The existence of these sorts of unilateral steps to force down the value of the dollar against the RMB is important because it establishes that the United States is not helpless in its negotiations with China. If there were sufficient determination to bring down the value of the dollar, then the United States could pursue one of these channels.

In the real world, the sort of currency war that these measures might imply would never materialize. If the United States were prepared to take unilateral measures to push down the value of the dollar, then China's government would almost certainly look to negotiate an increase in the value of its currency. It would inevitably demand concessions in other areas, but it is difficult to imagine China insisting on maintaining a low value for its currency as a fundamental principle. After all, it is not being asked to cede territory to the United States.

---

69 This route was first outlined in Gagnon and Hufbauer (2011).

70 Another possible route would be to have the U.S. government buy up huge amounts of futures of RMB in derivative markets. This could also have the effect of pushing up the value of the RMB in spot markets as wealthy Chinese and Chinese corporations attempted to hold RMB off the spot market to take advantage of selling them at higher prices in future markets.

Know how the game is played

At the end of the day, the U.S. Treasury has enormous ability to influence the value of the dollar. It is certainly capable of forcing the dollar down against the Chinese RMB and other important currencies, if this is a major goal of economic policy. So far, a lower-valued dollar has not made the cut. A high-valued dollar is in the interest of the financial industry and other powerful actors, and so the Treasury Department has not pursued a lower-valued dollar as major goal in negotiations with China or anyone else.

To this point, there has been little pressure to pursue a lower-valued dollar. The general public and many progressives are profoundly confused on this issue, as with so many others. We tend to view a high dollar as a point of pride, and feel it would be a humiliation if the dollar were to fall in value, or, even worse, lose its standing as the world's preeminent currency.

Deficit hawks, for example, routinely warn that a drop in the value of the dollar is a possible outcome of the failure to reduce the deficit. In fact, the standard economic models predict that a drop in the dollar is one of the outcomes of succeeding in the reduction of the deficit. This should be a desired outcome of a deficit-reduction policy, as net exports would displace government spending or consumption in generating demand.

In the case of the Treasury's power over the dollar, as with the Fed's control of short-term interest rates and its power to hold Treasury assets, progressives and the larger public are profoundly confused. There are few areas that are more important in determining economic outcomes, yet they are hardly in the debate. This is sort of like playing football without knowing that the way to score points is to get the ball into the other team's end zone. It's hard to win when you don't know how the game is played.

Chapter 8

Trade in an Overvalued-Dollar World

Combining a U.S. trade policy that encourages firms to move production abroad and a Treasury policy that overvalues the dollar is comparable to blowing up a levee and shoving ordinary workers into the current. The overvalued dollar directly handicaps U.S.-made products in international competition by making imports relatively cheap and exports relatively expensive. Trade deficits are the result, and they appear in the sectors of the economy that are exposed to international competition.

It just so happens that the sectors that have been subjected to international competition through trade agreements – first and foremost manufacturing – disproportionately employ non-college-educated workers. The loss of relatively good-paying jobs for workers without college degrees puts downward pressure not only on the wages of manufacturing workers but on the wages of all workers without college degrees.

Alternative dollar and trade policies could relieve the pressure on wages, and state-level policy measures and even private initiatives could potentially circumvent the regressive currency and trade policies at the national level.

As a practical matter, it will be difficult politically to alter dollar policy so that the value of the dollar is brought down to a level that is consistent with balanced trade. Dollar policy is conducted outside any arena in which the public has much say.

However, it should be possible to restructure the contours of trade policy so that more than just manufacturing workers are subject to international competition. Trade can be restructured in such a way that the most highly educated and highly paid workers are forced to compete against lower-paid counterparts from the developing world, by making it easier for foreign-born professionals to work in the United States and for U.S. residents to go abroad to receive highly skilled services.

This policy shift would have a direct, positive outcome, since forcing down the wages of the most highly paid workers would reduce the costs of goods and services they produce, thereby raising the real wage to all other workers.

Bringing the threat of international competition to the most highly paid workers would also be beneficial for the future of U.S. dollar policy. A high dollar would then put downward pressure on the pay of doctors and lawyers and other high-paid workers and increase their risk of job loss. It is a safe bet that these powerful constituencies would act as important lobbies pushing for a lower-valued dollar.

In effect, subjecting these highly paid workers to international competition would also push them into the current created by the overvalued dollar. Disempowered manufacturing workers are not in a position to have much impact on the value of the dollar. But if large numbers of doctors and lawyers suddenly saw their incomes threatened by imported services made cheap by an overvalued dollar, these professionals would likely be far more effective in lobbying to bring the dollar down to a sustainable level.

A lower dollar would be an important side benefit of pushing these groups of more highly educated workers into the current where ordinary workers have been treading water for nearly three decades. While the United States is likely to be able to borrow substantial amounts of money from foreign investors long into the future, it is not going to be able to run trade deficits equal to 5 to 6 percent of GDP indefinitely. Switching back to domestic production at some point is likely to be a costly process, since in many cases the U.S. now lacks capacity to meet its domestic demand. This switch would likely involve some supply disruptions and higher prices.

However, the shift toward more domestic production will be more painful the longer it is delayed. Each year we lose more physical capacity in key areas, while unemployed workers lose their skills. Making the adjustment sooner rather than later, and bringing trade closer to balance, will help to get the economy on a sustainable growth path with less disruption.

The simple act of pushing more dollars overseas helps to increase pressure on the dollar. Other things equal, spending tens or hundreds of billions of dollars each year buying the services of foreign professionals will directly lower the value of the dollar and improve the competitive position of U.S. manufacturing.

Alternatively, countries that peg their currency against the dollar may opt to increase their purchases to offset this effect, but this will make their pegging policy even more expensive than it already is. These countries already stand to lose large amounts of money on their dollar holdings; if we start buying professional services from abroad, they will stand to lose even more. There is presumably a limit to how much money China and other developing countries are prepared to lose subsidizing the purchases of consumers in the United States.[71]

The economics and politics of beating up professionals

The idea of deliberately trying to reduce the wages of physicians, lawyers, and other relatively high-paid professionals may seem perverse to many progressives. After all, these people make good salaries, but they are not the really big winners from the upward redistribution of the last three decades. Besides, for many progressives some of our best friends (including economists) are in these highly paid professions.

But several important points on this issue are poorly understood. First, everyone's salary is a cost to someone else. Paying our doctors twice as

---

71 When other countries buy up U.S. government bonds or other dollar-based assets to prop up the dollar, they are in effect subsidizing our purchases of their exports. The higher dollar makes their exports cheaper. However, since they are likely to get paid back in dollars that are worth less than the dollars they bought (because the value of the dollar declines) they will take a loss on their dollar assets. This loss is the cost of the subsidy to these countries.

much as those in other wealthy countries, which is roughly what we do, has the same impact on the living standards of non-doctors as if we imposed a tax of $100 billion a year (about $300 per person) to hand each doctor in the country a $100,000 check. A policy of taxing truck drivers and school teachers so that doctors' pay can average more than $200,000 a year would strike almost anyone as outrageous, but policies that protect U.S. doctors from effective competition with their foreign counterparts have the same effect.

As a practical matter, highly paid professionals tend to be conservative, especially on economic issues, and so measures that reduce their pay would have political as well as economic benefits. In addition to increasing the real income of nonprofessionals, lower pay for professionals would reduce their political power (less money, less power). It might also cause many of these professionals to become less conservative when they see that their lives can be made every bit as insecure as the lives of an auto or construction worker. While it is true that excessive compensation of doctors and lawyers is dwarfed by the extremes of corporate CEOs and Wall Street financiers, doctor and lawyer pay is nonetheless a substantial drain on the incomes of ordinary workers. A progressive agenda cannot support protectionist measures that continue to redistribute income upward to professionals.

Of course, measures designed to expose highly paid professionals to more competition will inevitably impact lower-paid workers within the same and related sectors. For example, a policy that facilitates medical trade (patients traveling internationally to receive medical services) will reduce demand not only for physicians but also for a wide range of workers in health care.

There is a view among many progressives that we have to structure our policies so that they don't harm anyone we care about. Yet, as a practical matter this is not possible. If we think that we have somehow protected all the affected parties, it is almost certainly because we have not fully considered the impact of the policy. For example, suppose we build a new airport or highway. These are great job-creating projects, but a new airport is likely to take away business and jobs from existing airports. Similarly, a new road will divert traffic from existing roads, and gas stations, motels, and stores along the older routes will lose sales.

Even if we create special funds to compensate affected workers, as has been proposed for coal miners in the case of restrictions on greenhouse gas emissions, the money must come from somewhere. The taxes needed to pay such displaced workers will lead to some job loss. The conservatives' argument about taxes having a negative impact on employment is generally true, though they typically overstate the size of the effect.

The point is that almost any policy that progressives want to promote will have losers among people whom we care about (the non-rich). That we choose to remain ignorant of those who lose out economically does not mean they don't exist. Ignorance is never good policy. We have to accept that there will be some losses and hardship and try to structure the economy in a way that ensures that those paying the cost will have other employment opportunities, and we need to structure the social safety net in a way that ensures those affected will be able to maintain a decent standard of living through any transition period.

If the right were as concerned about ensuring that no one in its ranks was ever harmed by its policies, it would oppose reductions in tax rates on the wealthy, since lower rates on high earners harm the accounting firms that specialize in creating tax dodges. Conservatives support policies that hurt particular segments of the business community all the time, but their expectation is that, on average, these policies will make the wealthy even wealthier. If progressives don't have the same attitude, then we should just acknowledge that we are playing games and not doing serious politics. That strategy is guaranteed to lose.

The bizarre logic of the trade ideologues

There is a peculiar view among the "free trade" lobby that somehow workers in the United States, because it is a wealthy country, should not be doing manufacturing work. Rather, we should all be employed in professional jobs that require college or even advanced degrees.

While the desire to see U.S. workers obtain more education and move up the skill ladder is commendable, the logic in the argument is warped. The reason that the United States loses manufacturing jobs to the developing world is that, with the same machinery and infrastructure, workers in the developing world can be every bit as productive as U.S. workers. But because they live in much poorer countries, workers in the developing world are willing to work for a fraction of the pay. As a result, auto workers with pay and benefit packages reaching $40 to $50 an hour can find themselves competing with workers in China or Mexico who receive pay and benefits less than a tenth as much.

However, the developing countries are also generating a workforce of skilled professionals who are prepared to work for much less money than their counterparts in the United States. Many Chinese engineers, computer programmers, and architects are every bit as skilled and creative as their counterparts in the United States, but they are willing to work for salaries that are a fifth or a tenth as much because they live in a poor country.

There is no logic whatsoever in the view that somehow the United States will remain dominant in highly skilled occupations, exporting the services produced in these areas to the rest of the world while importing manufactured goods from the rest of the world. It is perhaps a racist conception to believe that workers in the developing world somehow lack the capacity to compete effectively in skilled professions with people in the United States.

This view is especially bizarre given that many of the people who fill jobs in areas like computer engineering, conventional engineering, and other technical fields in the United States are of Indian or Chinese ancestry or are immigrants from these countries. To imagine that the United States can maintain an advantage over these countries in international trade involving these occupations would require a view that these engineers and designers can be effective when working in Silicon Valley or Seattle but suddenly become 80 or 90 percent less efficient if they return to their home countries or the countries of their forebears.

The United States is destined to import major quantities of highly paid professional services in the decades ahead, just as it now imports major quantities of manufactured goods. The argument for the benefit from these imports is the same as the argument for the benefit of importing manufactured goods: it allows us to buy these items at lower prices than if we relied on domestic production. This frees up income to purchase other goods and services, making us richer and increasing growth.

This is the nearly two-hundred-year-old argument for comparative advantage. It just turns out that the comparative advantages for the United States will not be where many economists and policy analysts believe they will be. Our advantage will not be exclusively in highly skilled professional services, although we will undoubtedly continue to have a large sector of our economy devoted to these activities. It is likely that the United States will end up producing in a wide range of sectors for both its domestic market and exports. In addition to highly paid professional services, this mix will also include tourism (an important growth sector for exports) and of course manufacturing.[72]

The outlook for currency policy

As noted in Chapter 4, the Clinton administration began to promote an overvalued dollar when Robert Rubin took over as Treasury secretary. The Treasury's direction of the IMF bailout of the East Asian countries following the 1997 financial crisis put muscle behind this policy. While the dollar has come down considerably from the peaks hit at the end of the 1990s, it must come down much further to close the United States' chronic trade imbalance (**Figure 8-1**).

---

72 Tourism in the United States by foreigners is treated as an export in the national income accounts. In effect people from abroad come to the United States to buy services from the industry. These purchases have largely the same impact on the economy as if the services could be packaged and shipped overseas as physical products.

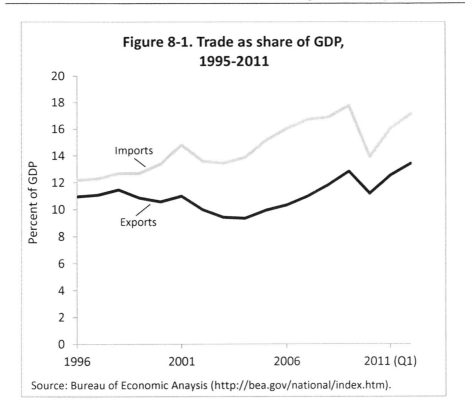

Figure 8-1. Trade as share of GDP, 1995-2011

Source: Bureau of Economic Anaysis (http://bea.gov/national/index.htm).

Both the Bush and Obama administrations have tolerated moderate declines in the value of the dollar, but neither has opted to push for a lower dollar as a matter of policy. Given the powerful interests who benefit from an overvalued dollar, most importantly the financial industry, it is unlikely that any president will deliberately push for a lower-valued dollar in the near future.

This means that we should expect that the dollar will continue to be overvalued for some time to come. It may trend downward but, barring a major change in the constellation of power in the country, the interest groups pushing to maintain an overvalued dollar are likely to continue to get their way. This means that in designing policy, we can take an overvalued dollar as a given.

Trade policy and the employment mix

The reason that the overvalued dollar leads to an upward redistribution of income and disproportionately hurts workers without college degrees is that it has been a deliberate goal of trade policy to subject these workers to international competition. The main objective of trade deals like NAFTA is to make it as easy as possible for manufacturing firms to relocate their operations to other countries. The trade deals' success can be measured by the more than five million manufacturing jobs lost (almost one-third of total manufacturing jobs) in the last 15 years.

Large-scale national campaigns organized to counter this trade policy over the last two decades have garnered considerable grassroots support and to a large extent have won over public opinion. Polls generally show that the public opposes NAFTA-type trade deals and sees them as a threat to jobs.[73]

These campaigns have had some success in slowing the Clinton-Bush-Obama trade agenda. Most of the bilateral trade deals have been delayed for years, and the Doha round of the World Trade Organization has now been delayed for more than a decade. To make trade deals more palatable to the U.S. public, negotiators have sought to include labor rights and other provisions that might reduce the negative impact that the deals would have on manufacturing employment in the United States and improve conditions for workers in our trading partners.

However, labor rights and worker protection provisions would have at best a marginal effect on reversing the extent to which trade policy redistributes income upward. As a result of current trade policy, U.S. manufacturers already have access to a vast pool of relatively low-paid workers in China, India, and elsewhere in the developing world. It will make little difference if they can also get access to low-cost labor in Colombia or Panama as a result of a new trade agreement.

It is almost inconceivable that this access to low-paid workers in the developing world, having once been granted, would be taken away by canceling or substantially altering existing trade pacts. And so, for the foreseeable future U.S. manufacturing workers will be forced to compete with

---

73 See for example Pew Research Center (2010).

the lowest-paid workers anywhere in the world and be disadvantaged further by an overvalued currency.

If we cannot restore protection to less-educated workers or reduce the value of the dollar to a sustainable level, we can at least redesign trade policy so as to place highly educated, high-cost workers – doctors, lawyers, dentists, etc. – into direct competition with their low-paid counterparts in the developing world. The key to such an effort would be to identify the factors that make it difficult for qualified professions from the developing world, or even from other wealthy countries, to practice their professions in the United States. In other words, we would seek to eliminate the barriers to a free flow of professionals into the United States in the same way that NAFTA sought to eliminate the obstacles to manufacturers relocating their operations in Mexico.

These barriers take a variety of forms, immigration policy being one. Since the provision of professional services is generally facilitated by the professional being physically located in the United States, restrictions on immigration effectively serve as restrictions on free trade in these services. While restaurants and construction companies have little to fear from not following the law in hiring immigrant employees, a hospital would risk serious sanctions if it hired doctors without the appropriate visas, even if the doctors met U.S. licensing standards.[74]

Getting trade agreements that allow free trade in professional services, and thereby put downward pressure on the wages of those at the top end of the labor market and reduce the cost of the services they provide to less-educated workers, will be a tough sell. The immediate obstacle is that these professionals are extremely powerful interest groups, wielding their influence both directly, through organizations like the American Medical Association and American Bar Association, which can be counted on to lobby against measures that increase the exposure of their members to international competition, and indirectly, through their control of public debate.

The categories of professional workers who are most protected from international competition overlap hugely with the categories of workers who write and report the news, staff congressional offices, and teach at colleges and universities. They are the people who shape the debate over policy issues like

---

74 Freeman (2003).

trade. And they use their control over this debate to prevent the notion of increased international competition in professional services from entering public debate.

In the mid-1990s there was a debate over efforts to tighten restrictions on the number of foreign medical residents entering the United States. The two sides in the debate were the physicians' organizations, who contended that foreign-born doctors were driving down the wages of doctors born in the United States, and community health groups, who argued that foreign-born doctors were serving underserved areas like rural areas, places where native-born doctors did not want to practice.[75]

Remarkably, no one was cited in this debate who gave the standard economists' argument that increasing the number of qualified foreign-born doctors in the country would drive down the wages of native-born doctors. This outcome would be good for the economy, since it would reduce the cost of medical care to patients, but the argument was not on the radar screens of the people reporting on the issue because the idea that reducing the wages of doctors could be positive is simply an alien notion.

While reporters and their editors understand completely how reducing the wages of retail clerks, auto workers, and school teachers can provide savings to consumers or taxpayers, they have difficulty applying the same logic to the pay of highly educated professionals. This disconnect likely stems from the fact that they are closely connected and identify with these professionals. Probably someone in their immediate family is a highly paid professional. They live in the same neighborhoods as doctors and lawyers; their kids go to school with the children of doctors and lawyers. For reporters and editors, highly paid professionals are friends and relatives, not people to be viewed as a cost of production.

The extent to which this class controls public debate makes it difficult to organize efforts to change policy. When almost every written and broadcast news story conceals the ways in which policy is designed to transfer income from ordinary workers to the most highly paid professionals, it raises the policy bar considerably, and it makes it difficult for most of us to even

---

75 The "problem" of too many foreign doctors entering the country is discussed in Sun (1996) and Pear (1997).

conceptualize what it is taking place.

Of course, consumers also have personal relationships with professionals. Patients usually like their doctors; otherwise they would get a different doctor if they had the option. Most patients do not want to force their doctors to take a big cut in pay, especially since patients generally are not covering the bulk of the cost themselves, but instead have it covered by a private insurer or the government.

Patients might view the matter differently if they were told that an average family of four is effectively paying a tax of $1,200 a year to allow doctors in the United States to enjoy higher living standards than doctors in other wealthy countries.[76] The savings from eliminating these excess physician salaries far outweigh the revenue to be gained from ending the Bush tax cuts on the wealthy (**Figure 8-2**).

---

76 Physicians in the United States earn on average more than $200,000 a year, compared to close to $100,000 a year in western European countries and Japan (Congressional Research Service, 2007). With 950,000 doctors in the United States, the savings if doctors in the U.S. were paid the same amount as in other countries is roughly $95 billion a year (Figure 8-2 assumes that this number grows in step with the economy), which is roughly $300 per person or $1,200 for a family of four. It is worth noting that a much higher share of doctors in the U.S. are specialists, who require more years of training, and therefore command higher salaries than family practitioners, than in most other wealthy countries. It is not clear that the greater number of specialists improves the quality of care, but it is likely that they are used in the United States in instances in which family practitioners would suffice. This sort of rent-seeking, with specialists inserting themselves into situations where their skills are not necessary, is exactly what would be expected when government interventions obstruct the normal workings of the market.

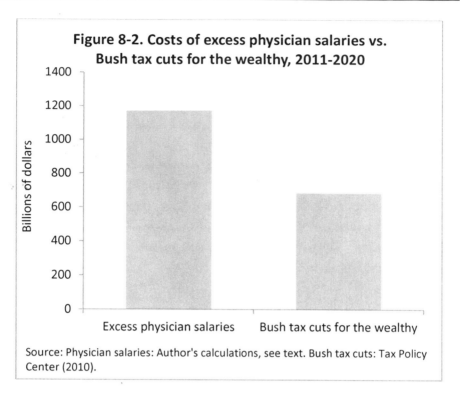

Figure 8-2. Costs of excess physician salaries vs. Bush tax cuts for the wealthy, 2011-2020

Billions of dollars

Excess physician salaries   Bush tax cuts for the wealthy

Source: Physician salaries: Author's calculations, see text. Bush tax cuts: Tax Policy Center (2010).

It is essential that people understand that the income of professionals is a cost to them, and that immigration and trade policies that restrict access to lower-cost alternatives is government intervention in the market. Conservatives understand fully that the pay of an ordinary worker is money out of their pockets, which is why they are so eager to use the levers of government to reduce it. However, few progressives seem to recognize the symmetry in the relationship: the money that goes to high-income individuals is money out of everyone else's pocket. This should be about as simple as it gets but, due to the bias in policy discussions, we rarely hear this obvious point.

Economists are almost completely useless in this respect because, like reporters and news editors, they belong to the same class of highly paid professionals. As a result, they bristle at the idea that anyone would apply trade theory to educated, accomplished people like themselves.[77]

Economists have also been known to put forward the "Mexican Avocado Theory of International Trade." Under this theory, going to the grocery store and finding an avocado that was grown in Mexico is proof that the United States has free trade in agricultural products. This is obviously an absurd extrapolation. The United States has a wide range of restrictions on importing agricultural products; the fact that it is still possible to buy a Mexican avocado proves nothing. Yet economists often apply this theory to convince themselves that we have free trade in professional services. For example, when an economist encounters a professional who is foreign born (e.g., the family's physician or the economist in the next office), the economist assumes there are no restrictions on foreign-born professions working in the United States.

As a practical matter, almost no trade barrier ever leads to an absolute prohibition on trade. The point of barriers is that they raise the cost of importing items, causing us to import less of the protected item. The barriers to foreign-born professionals working in the United States do not completely exclude them from working in the United States; they simply make it more difficult than necessary. A certain number of intelligent hard-working foreigners will overcome these barriers in order to take advantage of the better conditions enjoyed by professionals in the United States than in their home countries. However, the more typical foreign-born professional may not be prepared to make the necessary sacrifices. This leads to losses both for them and for consumers in the United States.

An economist once said to me, for the purpose of dismissing the notion that there were barriers preventing foreign-born economists from working in the United States, that "all the best economists I know were born

---

77 Once while on a panel discussing trade policy, I made a reference to the effort in the 1990s to tighten industry requirements in order to reduce the number of foreign-born doctors who could practice in this country. My fellow panelist, a prominent trade economist, said that he didn't know anything about the restriction and acted as though it had nothing to do with his line of work. This should have been a hugely embarrassing admission for a trade economist. There is far more money at stake in the salaries of doctors in the United States than in the various trade agreements that have been the topic of much political debate, or in the few instances in which the United States has imposed special trade restrictions (e.g., the Buy America provision of the stimulus) to assist a troubled industry.

in India." While this might well have been true, if the United States actually had free trade for economists then it is likely that the vast majority of the mediocre economists he knew would also have been born in India. It's not surprising that some of the best economists in India have been able to overcome the barriers to working in the United States. But if we actually had free trade, the typical economist in India would have the opportunity to work here too.

One of the misleading arguments often used to deny the existence of protectionist barriers that artificially inflate the salaries of professionals is to claim that foreign-born professionals are typically not trained to U.S. standards. This may be true in many cases, but it raises a chicken-and-egg question. If foreign-born professionals are largely excluded from working as professionals in the United States, why would they bother to train to U.S. standards? They would train to meet the standards in their home country. But if they knew there were an open door, offering the same opportunities as a professional born in New York or Los Angeles, then a huge number of foreign-born professionals would train to these standards. This is where trade agreements like NAFTA come in.

If the United States had wanted to open up professional services like medical care and the legal profession in the same way that it opened up trade in manufacturing goods, it would have written up clear guidelines for the standards that Mexicans doctors and lawyers would have to meet in order to have free access to practicing their professions in the United States. The agreement also would have established testing systems within Mexico (by U.S.-certified testers) that would allow Mexican professionals the convenience of obtaining the necessary certification in their home country before committing themselves to the expense and disruption of moving.

Once they obtained their certification, Mexican professionals would have the same opportunity to practice their profession in the United States as native-born professionals. [78] This would be a situation where both the

---

78 Those concerned about too many immigrants entering the country need not worry. There are about 4.5 million workers with doctorates or professional degrees in the United States. Even if foreign professionals equal to half this number entered the country over the next decade, the annual flow would total just 230,000 workers, or less than 20 percent of the projected flow of immigrants over the next decade. If there is a desire to keep the total

immigrant professionals and U.S. consumers come out as winners: the professionals would view themselves as better off, and the influx of a large number of qualified Mexican professionals would reduce the amount that people in the United States would have to spend on health care, legal fees, and a variety of other services.

It will be important to structure this policy so that Mexico also benefits from having its professionals work in the United States. A tax on these professionals' wages that was repatriated to Mexico for the first 10 years would likely total enough money to train several professionals for each one who goes to work in the United States. This arrangement can help to ensure that Mexico doesn't suffer a shortage of doctors or other skilled professionals because they have all gone to work in the United States.

Getting around federal trade policy

The irony of free trade is that the market actually favors progressive outcomes. If the barriers that protect the most highly paid professionals can be weakened or eliminated, the bulk of the population will benefit. Essentially, progressives should want a free market.

While it is simple to envision policy changes that would ensure that trade benefits the bulk of the population rather than simply redistributing income upward, as a practical matter such policies have no chance in Washington for the foreseeable future. There is no organized constituency arguing for a forward-thinking trade policy that would benefit those at the middle and bottom, and the debate is completely controlled by people who benefit from the status quo.

However, there are arenas beyond Washington that might be more favorable.

One place where the battle could be contested is at the level of state licensing. States license doctors, lawyers, and most other professionals. While the point of licensing is ostensibly to ensure the quality of the services being

---

flow of immigrants below some fixed level, then the number of people allowed to enter the country to work in construction, hotels, and restaurants can be reduced to offset the number of additional professionals entering the country.

provided and protect patients and other consumers, in reality professional groups use the process to protect their incomes. (Ask your state medical board how many doctors have lost their licenses because of malpractice over the last decade.)

It would be relatively easy to open up the licensing process to allow a far wider range of people to be admitted into the professions while still ensuring quality standards. For example, allowing doctors who have been licensed in countries with comparable standards to automatically be licensed in a given state could potentially give many more doctors the opportunity to practice in the state. Major hospitals, clinics, and other employers of large numbers of doctors ought to be natural allies in such a campaign, and insurers should welcome the opportunity to pay lower reimbursement schedules to doctors and other highly paid professionals.[79]

Businesses looking for attorneys and universities seeking teachers ought to welcome the opportunity to hire foreign lawyers and foreign professors who will work at much lower wages than the current workforce.

Outsourcing offers another means to take advantage of lower-cost professional services – just ask the manufacturers who have used outsourcing to employ workers at lower wages. In the case of medical care, the obvious mechanism is medical trade.[80] While it would not pay to go abroad for routine medical procedures (except for people living near the Canadian or Mexican borders), for more complex medical procedures, the savings can be so large as to cover travel expenses and an extended stay overseas for patients and their family members.

Table 8-1 compares the price of major medical procedures in India, Thailand, and Singapore with the price in the United States. The prices shown are taken from modern hospitals that have state-of-the-art medical technology

---

79 Employers are already aggressively following this approach with regard to foreign nurses, pushing to ease immigration restrictions in order to bring in ever-larger numbers of nurses with the explicit intent of lowering their wages. If this effort can be redirected toward doctors and others at the top of the pay ladder, then there is an opportunity for large economic gains that benefit nearly everyone.

80 Medical trade is often referred to as "medical tourism." This is an unfortunate term because it trivializes what could be a life-saving trip in which a patient goes overseas to get an essential medical procedure that he or she could not afford in the United States.

and doctors who are trained to Western standards. There is no reason to believe that using these facilities would compromise the quality of the care received by the patient, although traveling halfway around the world to receive medical care is obviously a major inconvenience.

Table 8-1
Comparative costs of medical procedures, by country

Procedure	U.S.	India	Thailand	Singapore
Heart valve replacement	$160,000	$9,000	$10,000	$12,500
Heart bypass	$130,000	$10,000	$11,000	$18,500
Spinal fusion	$62,000	$5,500	$7,000	$9,000
Angioplasty	$57,000	$11,000	$13,000	$13,000
Hip replacement	$43,000	$9,000	$12,000	$12,000
Knee replacement	$40,000	$8,500	$10,000	$13,000
Hysterectomy	$20,000	$3,000	$4,500	$6,000

AMA-OMSS Governing Council (2007).

While no one should be forced to go overseas to get care (unfortunately, some uninsured are already in this situation), insurers could nevertheless provide incentives to patients to get their treatment at a lower-cost facility overseas. By sharing the savings, insurers could vastly increase the number of people seeking lower-cost care abroad. If an insurer can save $110,000 when a patient receives a heart bypass operation in Singapore rather than the United States, it could share perhaps $50,000 of the savings with the patient. Both come out ahead.

Of course, ensuring the quality of care in facilities in other countries would be vital. An international licensing organization that could certify the quality of facilities in foreign countries could be valuable in this respect. There would also be the need for clear legal rules to allow patients redress in the event of malpractice. Ideally, the host countries would tax medical trade and use the revenue to build up their health care systems to the benefit of their own populations.

State and local governments can advance the growth of medical trade by taking the lead themselves. They can offer insurance plans to their own workers that allow patients to share in the savings from having major medical procedures performed in overseas facilities. They can also secure substantial savings by allowing for foreign medical care in state Medicaid programs. If governmental units take the lead, private-sector employers are likely to follow. Also, large governmental units may be better situated than most private companies to ensure that high-quality care is provided to the first large groups of patients that go overseas for medical care.

State governments can carry through most of the legal and regulatory changes necessary to facilitate large-scale medical trade, and as the industry gained size it would reduce demand for medical services within the United States. Salaries within the industry, especially among the most highly paid professionals, would fall,[81] as would the cost of health care.

Traveling overseas for medical care may seem a perverse alternative to simply fixing the domestic health care system in the United States. It is. But as the debate over President Obama's health care reform bill made clear, there is no realistic prospect of fixing the domestic health care system given the current distribution of power in the United States.

From the beginning, the Obama administration negotiated deals with most of the major interest groups in the industry: the pharmaceutical companies, the insurance companies, and the physicians' lobbies. This strategy ensured that the final product would not be a plan that substantially reduced the profits/incomes of any of the big actors. And if the incomes of the big actors are not reduced, then health care will eventually be unaffordable to individuals and the government.

It's possible to criticize the Obama administration's approach as a moral failure, but this is irrelevant. Officials in high office are always going to respond first and foremost to political concerns. President Obama is much less likely to face serious political consequences from having pushed a health care

---

81 The downward pressure will be greatest for those at the top for the simple reason that these people enjoy the greatest economic rents. As much as physicians may complain about their inadequate pay, they have few choices since they are already at the top of the pay scale. Specialists earning $300,000 a year have few comparable employment options. If their pay were cut to $180,000 they would not do better by leaving medicine and going to work as clerks in a shoe store. On the other hand, those lower down the pay ladder have less to lose by leaving their professions. If pay were cut substantially for nurses, nurses' assistants, lab technicians, and other lower- and middle-paying occupations, these jobs would more likely go unfilled.

plan that depended on deals with the major interest groups in the industry than he would have had he pushed a plan that threatened these groups' incomes.

By contrast, President Obama would have faced serious political risks had he taken the more progressive route. Unless advocates of more progressive health care reform can bring some symmetry to the political calculus, there is little hope that President Obama or any other elected official in a position to effect change will go the progressive route.

It is nevertheless difficult to envision a scenario in which the political balance moves much in a progressive direction on this issue in the foreseeable future. If this is the case, then fixing the domestic health care system within the current political framework is not a viable path. There have to be ways to alter the structure of the debate so that more extensive reform becomes possible.

The experience of the U.S. auto industry provides an interesting, if painful, lesson in this respect. The control of the U.S. auto market by the Big Three automakers through the late 1970s allowed for secure employment with good wages and benefits for a large group of workers with limited education. Moreover, the factories provided a solid tax base for the governments where auto plants were located. Several generations of auto workers were able to attain a comfortable middle-class status. They were able to raise their children in decent neighborhoods, send them to good schools, and pay for their college.

The downside of this picture is that the limited competition among the Big Three meant that the industry became complacent. It produced cars of mediocre quality, and it was slow to innovate. Foreign competition changed that. This first became a major issue for the auto industry in the early 1980s, when high oil prices sent consumers to look for more fuel-efficient imports. The high dollar of the mid-1980s provided a large cost advantage to imports, which placed further pressure on the domestic manufacturers.

The pressure from import competition continued to build through the 1990s and into the last decade, eventually leading to the bankruptcy of General Motors and Chrysler. As a result of these bankruptcies and the continuing pressure on industry profits, the United Auto Workers (UAW) accepted large cuts in pay and benefits. The new starting wage for union auto workers under the most recent contract is just $14 per hour, an amount that would certainly not provide sufficient income to maintain a middle-class lifestyle and put children through college.

Gains in living standards that the UAW built up over many decades were wiped out when the survival of the domestic industry was called into question. However, it is important to recognize that this victory over the auto workers was not the result of a head-on confrontation. Rather, it was the result of several decades in which their position was eroded by the growing presence of foreign manufacturers with lower-cost structures.

The same sort of structures can be put in place to weaken the power of the domestic health care industry. Buying lower-cost health care services elsewhere will gradually erode demand for services from domestic health care providers in the same way as the growing presence of foreign manufacturers in the U.S. market eroded the demand for U.S. cars. However the big losers in this case will be highly paid physicians, not middle-income workers.

A side benefit of people taking advantage of lower-cost health care in other countries is that it would undermine much of the mythology that has grown around the U.S. health care system. Politicians who make grand statements about how the United States has the best health care system in the world should be greeted with howls of laughter, because it is obviously untrue. Yet they tend to get away with it. If a substantial portion of the population had direct experience with the health care systems in other countries, politicians would have to choose their words more carefully.

While state governments can attempt to remove barriers to private insurers taking advantage of other countries' health systems, there is a relatively simple measure that could be implemented at the national level. The federal government could allow Medicare beneficiaries to buy into the health care systems of countries with longer life expectancies than the United States. Per-person health care costs in other wealthy countries average less than half as much as in the United States. In fact, the bulk of the long-term deficit problem at the center of budget debates stems from the fact that this enormous gap in per-person health care costs is projected to grow over time (**Figure 8-3**).

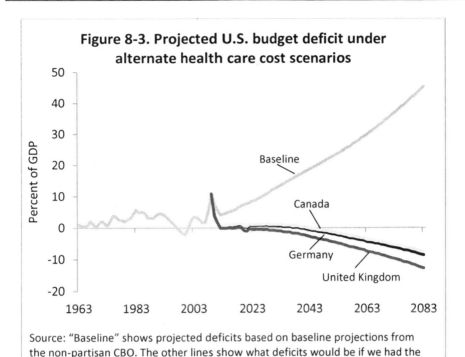

Figure 8-3. Projected U.S. budget deficit under alternate health care cost scenarios

Source: "Baseline" shows projected deficits based on baseline projections from the non-partisan CBO. The other lines show what deficits would be if we had the same per person health care costs as those countries. For additional details, see http://www.cepr.net/calculators/hc/hc-calculator.html.

This big cost difference means that there are enormous potential savings from allowing Medicare beneficiaries to receive their care in Canada, Germany, or other wealthy countries rather than in the United States. **Figure 8-4** shows the potential benefit to Medicare beneficiaries, and dual beneficiaries of Medicare and Medicaid, if they got their care in Canada and split the savings with the government. The gains to beneficiaries would easily dwarf the average Social Security benefit in the decades ahead, according to the government's projections. Splitting the savings would both provide beneficiaries with a substantial boost to their retirement income and allow the government to address its deficit.[82]

---

82 This policy is outlined in Baker and Rho (2009). Since many Medicare beneficiaries are enrolled in the Medicaid program, the potential savings per beneficiary can run into the tens of thousands of dollars a year, using current projections.

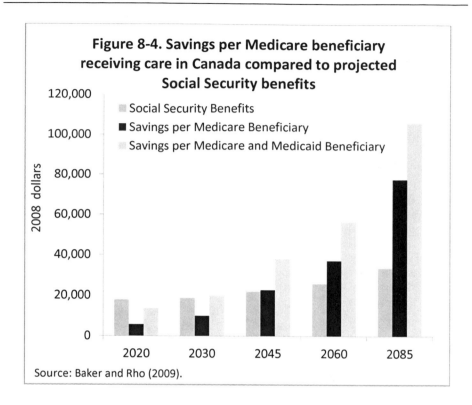

Figure 8-4. Savings per Medicare beneficiary receiving care in Canada compared to projected Social Security benefits

Source: Baker and Rho (2009).

Allowing for international Medicare vouchers does require action from Congress, which is an enormous obstacle. However, the usual conservative arguments against any policy that might benefit ordinary working-class people at the expense of the wealthy hold no water in this case. The proposal does nothing to disrupt the existing system of health care in the United States. Plus, it saves the government money and gives people a choice – exactly the sort of policy that any honest conservative would favor. The only real argument against the policy is that domestic medical and pharmaceutical industries would lose money. In other words, conservatives' inevitable opposition to the policy will illuminate the fact that the right's goals have nothing to do with small government or promoting the market and everything to do with redistributing income upward.

Free trade in professions other than medical care

It should be easy to make progress toward free trade in highly paid professions beyond medical care and dentistry, since a smaller share of most others' work is likely to be location-specific. To a substantial extent, the transfer of services overseas is already taking place. In the case of software design, the United States is already a large net importer of software from India.[83] The deficit is virtually certain to grow rapidly in the years ahead, with designers in the United States still receiving pay packages 5-10 times greater than their counterparts in India. And it's far cheaper to send a computer program from India to the United States than to ship a car from the other side of the world.

The story is similar in engineering. A vast pool of low-cost engineering labor in India and China is willing to work for wages that are far lower than those that engineers receive in the United States, and so governments and private corporations will be able to save large sums by substituting engineers in these countries for engineers in the United States. The same is true for architects, biomedical researchers, and workers in most other professional and technical fields.

Outsourcing top management

It is not just highly paid professionals who work for less in other countries than they do in the United States. The CEOs and other top executives of major corporations in Europe and Asia generally receive much lower pay – to the tune of millions of dollars each – than do American executives.

This pay gap suggests the possibility of large gains to the U.S. economy and to groups of workers who are not in top corporate management from taking advantage of lower-paid top management at foreign companies wherever possible. The best recent example is the bailout of Chrysler, which saved the jobs of tens of thousands of manufacturing workers both at Chrysler itself and in its chain of suppliers. Chrysler's rescue was accomplished in part

---

83 The Commerce Department reported that in 2009 the United States imported $8.9 billion of business and professional services from India, while it exported only $1.3 billion (http://www.bea.gov/international/xls/tab5a.xls).

by outsourcing top management and engineering roles to Fiat, an Italian car manufacturer.

U.S.-based companies have been telling the public for years that their first obligation is to their bottom lines and not to the U.S. economy. This may not be entirely true – they seem to be operating to serve the interests of top management first and foremost – but corporate managers are being truthful when they tell the public that they should not be expected to operate in the national interest.

But on the flip side, the public has no patriotic obligation to favor contracts with U.S.-based companies simply because the companies have a headquarters in the United States. Where foreign-based companies like Fiat can offer lower costs, at least in part because their executives are lining their pockets much less amply at the company's expense, progressives should jump at the opportunity to bring them on board. And if U.S.-based companies with bloated executive compensation packages are frozen out of public contracts at the local, state, and federal level, it will be a good thing. We should care that work is done in the United States, not whether we support an overpaid U.S.-based CEO.

Chapter 9

Reining in Finance

The financial sector serves an essential economic purpose by channeling money from savers to those who want to borrow, whether to buy a home, start a business, or pay for a college education. An efficient, well-run financial sector accomplishes these tasks with the fewest possible resources, meaning that it employs a small share of the workforce and pays salaries comparable to those earned elsewhere in the economy.

This is not the financial sector that the United States has today. Our financial sector is hugely bloated, and it is a massive source of waste in the economy. Measured as a share of private-sector GDP, the financial sector more than quadrupled between 1975 and 2009.[84] The enormous expansion would be justifiable if it resulted in a better allocation of capital, so that promising start-ups, say, could more easily raise funds than they could in the 1960s. A better allocation of capital would also mean that hare-brained schemes like Pets.com or Webvan would be less likely to receive funding today than in prior decades. But neither seems to be the case, or at least not

---

84 These figures come from the Commerce Department's National Income and Product Accounts, Tables 6.2B and 6.2D. The securities and investment portion of private-sector employee compensation rose from 0.5 percent in 1975 (lines 55 and 89) to 2.4 percent in 2009 (lines 59 and 61).

obviously enough to justify the quadrupling of the sector as a share of GDP. Moreover, productivity growth, the most direct measure of the rate of innovation, was more rapid in the 1950s and 1960s than in the last two decades.

Another indication that the economy was being well-served by its booming financial sector would be that people felt more secure in their savings than they did four decades ago. Here again, the sector falls short. Not only have we experienced extraordinary volatility in the stock and housing markets over the last 15 years, but we are also less secure because we are far less likely today to have defined-benefit pensions at our workplaces. In the 1960s and 1970s, roughly half of all private-sector workers had a defined-benefit pension; by 2011 the share was less than 20 percent and falling.

The financial sector thrives on a huge amount of economic rent, which means it makes money through tax and regulatory arbitrage that provides no real benefit to society. For example, it became common in the 1980s and 1990s for government agencies like transit departments to sell off equipment, such as buses and subway cars, to private companies, and then lease it back. The logic of these deals is that the private company can take the depreciation on the equipment as a tax write-off, whereas as the state or local government agency cannot. The value of the tax break gets split between the company buying the equipment and the governmental agency selling it, and the bank or insurance company that worked out the deal gets a cut.

This sale/leaseback arrangement engineered a way for the federal government to subsidize the purchase of capital equipment through a tax benefit. This might be good policy, but it would be much more efficient if the law were simply changed to allow governments to take the tax deduction directly instead of going through this unnecessarily elaborate routine.

A similar scam, the "dead peasant" insurance policy, gained prominence when it was featured in Michael Moore's film, "Capitalism: A Love Story." A dead peasant policy is insurance purchased by a company on the lives of its lower-level employees. Wal-Mart reportedly purchased life insurance policies on 350,000 of its workers. Under these policies the company is the beneficiary and the employees generally do not even know that a policy has been taken out on their behalf. In fact, the relatives of employees typically will not know of the policy even after their family member has died.

Moore focused on the morbid nature of the policies – companies profit from the death of employees who never even knew they were insured. However, the fuller story is even more disturbing. Wal-Mart and other companies taking out dead peasant policies do not directly profit from the policies, in the sense that Aetna or some other major insurer is paying them back more in benefits than they paid in premiums. Insurers are not charities, or dummies.

Rather, the benefit is that dead peasant policies allow companies to control the timing of their earnings. If a company wants to show lower profits in 2011 for tax purposes or just smooth a growth rate, the dead peasant policy can be the perfect tool. The payment on 30,000 insurance policies in 2011 will be a deduction from profits in 2011. With a relatively large pool of insured workers, Wal-Mart can be reasonably confident of the rate at which they will die, and so it can count on collecting benefits that will boost profits in future years.

The result is that the dead peasant policy is in effect another financial instrument that allows corporations to adjust earnings in ways that minimize their tax liability.[85] And of course some brilliant finance people thought this one up, making themselves and their employer large amounts of money as a result. This is the sort of activity that has quadrupled the financial sector's share of the economy. It is not about allocating capital to its best uses or making savings more secure, it's about finding clever ways to rip off taxpayers, productive businesses, and other actors. The economy will benefit from having less of this sort of inefficient rent-seeking behavior. While this may have seemed like a radical assessment a decade ago, even the IMF now recognizes that there are substantial rents in the financial sector and that governments should adopt policies to reduce the sector's size.[86]

Tremendous waste in the financial sector is not the only justification for reducing its size. The sector has also been a major cause of instability. It fueled both the stock and housing bubbles, and restructuring it to make it less bubble-prone would be a huge boost to the economy.

---

85 Control over the timing of earnings may also be at the expense of shareholders. For example, this mechanism may make it easier for top executives to time earnings in ways that ensure that they will meet bonus targets.

86 IMF (2010).

Finally, the financial sector is potentially harmful simply because of its outsized political influence, which it marshals to support policies that stand in direct opposition to the interests of the bulk of the population. It favors very low inflation, even at the cost of higher unemployment, and prefers a high dollar so that it can be a bigger actor in international finance. In contrast, for workers a high dollar is a major subsidy to their foreign competitors.

For these reasons, reducing the size of the financial sector is both good economics and good politics. A smaller financial sector that is more directly focused on its economic function should be at or near the top of every progressive's agenda.

While it is good politics and good economics, what it is not is a battle between those wanting regulation and those wanting an unfettered market. The financial sector in its current form is heavily dependent on the government for its survival. The insurance provided by the Federal Deposit Insurance Corporation (FDIC) and comparable government insurers is certainly not a market mechanism, and it can subsidize bank excesses if it is given without proper regulation. [87] In addition, banks enjoy the back-up liquidity guarantees provided by the Federal Reserve Board.

The largest banks also have the implicit support of the government's too-big-to-fail policy. Virtually no one believes that the government would allow J.P. Morgan or Goldman Sachs to simply go bankrupt. As a result, these huge banks are able to borrow funds at a lower cost than their smaller rivals, an arrangement that amounts to a substantial subsidy from the government to these large banks. [88]

The elimination of these subsidies would be a genuine free-market approach, but the financial industry wants to maintain its insurance while removing restrictions that limit the risk to taxpayers. The banks' efforts do not represent a debate between those advocating an unfettered market and those who want government regulation. This is an argument with an industry that wants the taxpayers to provide it insurance but doesn't want to have to pay for the insurance and doesn't want to have any restrictions that prevent it from

87 Even in cases where deposit insurance is provided privately, there is still an expectation that the government will stand behind these insurers in a crisis, since the consequences of letting a major private bank insurance fund go bankrupt would be disastrous.
88 Baker and McArthur (2009).

raising the risk to taxpayers. In other words, the industry wants to set up a fireworks factory in its basement and not even pay the standard homeowners' insurance rate.

While there was considerable rhetoric about reforming the financial sector and reining in its abuses following the collapse of the housing bubble and the ensuing financial crisis, little about the industry has changed as a result of the Dodd-Frank financial reform bill. The industry is still dominated by too-big-to-fail institutions that are now bigger than ever as a result of crisis-induced mergers.

In principle, regulators have expanded resolution authority that gives them a non-bankruptcy alternative to address a Lehman or AIG-type situation in which a systemically important nonbank financial institution faces collapse. However, few believe that regulators would use resolution authority to allow a Goldman Sachs liquidation that left its uninsured creditors out in the cold. For this reason, the country's largest banks continue to be able to borrow at much lower interest rates than their smaller competitors. The basic story is simple: it's cheaper to borrow when the government co-signs your loans.

The progressive agenda on finance

In dealing with the financial industry progressives would do well to think like economists. We need the financial industry to connect borrowers with lenders in an efficient way, meaning that the industry uses as few resources as possible. A financial sector that employs few people is better than a financial sector that employs many people, at least if the smaller sector is as effective at connecting lenders and borrowers as the larger sector. An economy is efficient when it employs its resources in productive tasks. We do not need people shuffling financial assets back and forth in make-work projects.

Breaking up the big banks is a necessary part of financial reform for both political and economic reasons. As noted above, treating an institution as too-big-to-fail effectively amounts to a government subsidy to its top executives and shareholders. It is difficult to see any rationale for providing such a subsidy.

However, big banks are also politically powerful banks. The major Wall Street financial institutions have an extensive network of connections with the Treasury and the White House and key members of Congress — regardless of which party is in power — and they use these connections to defeat or dilute regulatory efforts that threaten their profitability. While other countries may have a tradition of an independent civil service that can effectively regulate large financial institutions, the United States does not. There is little reason to believe that regulators will be any more successful at standing up to the large banks in the future than they have been in the past.

The technical issues associated with breaking up large banks are not nearly as difficult as the banks' defenders have argued. The government does not actually have to break up the banks; it just has to tell the banks to break themselves up. This point is important because it would undoubtedly be difficult for regulators to figure out how to best disassemble a J.P. Morgan or Bank of America into manageable chunks.

However, there is no reason for regulators to ever be in that position. They need only set size limits to be reached by specific dates, with severe penalties for failing to meet the deadlines. For example, each of the six large banks could be given a deadline by which time it must have assets of less than $1 trillion, another deadline for getting its assets under $800 billion, a third for getting under $600 billion, etc. The bank would then face a penalty in the form of a tax on the assets it holds over the limit for the period of time it holds them. The top executives of these banks know the companies they manage and they know how to best divide the companies in a way that maximizes the value to shareholders.

In addition to reducing the size of the largest banks, we also need to re-introduce a Glass-Steagall-type separation between insured banking activities and speculative transactions. The public interest requires that we ensure the soundness of the banks that maintain the system of payments, and this is why we have deposit insurance and the protections afforded by the Fed and the FDIC. There is no comparable interest in protecting institutions like investment banks and hedge funds that are engaged in more speculative activities, and so banks that benefit from deposit insurance should not be engaged in such activity.

This wall between banking and speculation was the intention behind the Volcker Rule that was included in the Dodd-Frank financial reform law of 2010. The Volcker Rule prohibits insured banks from trading on their own accounts. While this is consistent with the original intention of Glass-Steagall, it is not clear that it will be possible to enforce a narrow restriction like the Volcker Rule as opposed to a broader Glass-Steagall prohibition on combining commercial and investment banks.

The enforcement problem stems from defining trading on a bank's own account as opposed to trading on behalf of clients. Banks that act as market makers in stocks and other assets will inevitably take positions for periods of time, buying an asset from clients who want to sell and arranging the purchase of an asset to fill orders for customers. Distinguishing trades that are necessary to this market-making role from trades transacted by the bank for its own gain will not be an easy job for regulators.

The public will always be at a disadvantage in this situation because the financial industry will heavily influence the rules set by regulators. The design of these sorts of rules requires specialized expertise in the nuts and bolts of the financial industry. Few people outside of the financial industry have this expertise. Since there are potentially tens of billions in profits at stake in the specifics of these rules, the industry is prepared to spend substantial sums to ensure that they are written in a way that is not overly restrictive. Comparable expertise on the other side is rare, and this creates a strong bias for regulators to adopt an industry-friendly position.

For this reason, a clear separation between conventional banking and investment banking, like the one imposed by Glass-Steagall, may be the only effective way to keep banks with insured deposits from taking excessive risks. It is worth noting that the repeal of Glass-Steagall did not contribute in any major way to the inflation of the housing bubble or the subsequent financial crisis. Most of the major investment banks did buy up commercial bank subsidiaries that fed them mortgages for securitization, but this was a minor part of the story. Investment banks acquired the vast majority of the junk loans they securitized during this period on the open market.

However, just because allowing banks with government-insured deposits to engage in speculative activity did not cause the last crisis does not mean it will not cause the next one. There is no obvious reason that a bank that receives government insurance for a substantial portion of its operations should be allowed to take excessive risks in its other operations. The banks argue that they will keep the insured and speculative portions of their operations strictly separate. If this is so, then why operate them both? There are no economies of scale or scope achieved by bringing them together under a single corporate roof.

Even the supposed convenience of providing customers with one-stop shopping, where they can bank, buy insurance, and invest in the stock market, does not hold water on closer inspection. If consumers really want to be able to conduct business in all three areas at the same time, there is nothing to prevent an independent insurer or brokerage house from sharing a building with a bank.

Securitization and mortgage mayhem

The collapse of Fannie Mae and Freddie Mac has left the future of housing finance wide open. Unfortunately, the solutions on the table are more likely to enrich the financial industry than promote homeownership.

Before considering the prospects for the reform of Fannie and Freddie, it is worth discussing the benefits of homeownership. Over the last seven decades, politicians from both parties have pushed homeownership as a ticket to the middle class. This view of homeownership ignores much evidence and shows sloppy thinking.

First, homeownership involves large transaction costs. The combination of realtors' fees, mortgage origination fees, inspection fees, and other costs associated with buying and selling a home are likely to push the combined purchase and sale costs to close to 10 percent of the home's price, or $20,000 on a $200,000 home. Averaged over a long period these costs will diminish, but for someone who lives in a home for five years or less they loom large. This means that anyone who is not in a stable employment or family situation in which they can expect to stay in the same place for five years or more would be best advised not to buy a home.

A second point is that home prices on average only rise with the overall rate of inflation. This means that owning a home is not necessarily a good investment. A standard 30-year fixed-rate mortgage is one way to effectively force people to save, since mortgage holders accumulate equity over time. However, other mechanisms for savings can offer higher returns. In many cases, people would be better off renting and placing money in a retirement fund than being a homeowner.

Third, homeownership can be a risky investment. This was not only true during the housing bubble, which made a home purchase an almost guaranteed losing investment at its peak, but also more generally. While in some areas home prices rise substantially more than inflation, in others they fall far behind inflation.

Furthermore, the prospect for home prices in many cases is likely to be highly correlated with the area's employment prospects. For example, home prices in Detroit have followed the ups and downs of the auto industry. The same is true for many other areas where a single industry or even a single employer dominates a city's economy. This creates a situation in which the value of a worker's major asset, his or her home, is dependent on the same forces that determine the health of the worker's employer.

Having your job and your home's value tied to the same thing is like putting all your retirement savings into the stock of the company you work for. If the company takes a downturn, you run the risk of losing both your job and most of your savings. This is roughly the situation faced by tens of thousands of unemployed homeowners in the Detroit area and hundreds of thousands around the country. They have lost their jobs and are also faced with the prospect of selling their homes at large losses.

While the specific situations that many workers find themselves in may have been unpredictable, the risk was 100 percent predictable. The idea that homeownership is somehow a secure investment immune to the ups and downs of the economy is nonsense. The fact that the downs are associated with periods of unemployment makes the risks even greater.

In spite of these cautions, one can still argue that the government has an interest in promoting homeownership as a way to provide secure housing and a mechanism for savings. However, this does not mean that homeownership is a sure ticket to the middle class or that more homeownership is always better than less.

The most obvious way that the government subsidizes homeownership is through the mortgage interest deduction. However, the deduction is an inefficient mechanism for helping low- and middle- income people buy homes because it is worth less to families in lower income brackets, many of whom do not even itemize their deductions. The overwhelming majority of the benefit goes to the upper-middle class and the wealthy. A simple way to increase the subsidy to lower-income families would be to change the deduction into a refundable tax credit of some amount (e.g., 15 percent). The additional cost could be covered by reducing the availability of the subsidy for higher-income homeowners. In any case, a credit for mortgage interest can be used to make the subsidy as large as is desired.

This point is important in the context of restructuring Fannie Mae and Freddie Mac, because having a government role in the mortgage financing process effectively amounts to a second source of subsidy to homeownership. It is not clear why it is necessary to create a second channel through which the government subsidizes homeownership. Fannie Mae's establishment in 1937 created a secondary market for mortgages, which ensured that banks in different regions could secure the necessary capital to issue new loans even if they had a large stock of mortgages. Fannie Mae was an important innovation that played a major role in promoting ownership in the 1940s, 1950s, and 1960s.

However, with a much more developed national financial system there is no obvious reason that the government needs to create a secondary mortgage market. Banks can both sell mortgages without government guarantees and tap the national (as opposed to regional) credit market to obtain additional deposits if they find themselves lacking money to lend.

In this context current proposals to recreate a Fannie/Freddie type system that would have the government guarantee mortgage-backed securities seem to be more a subsidy to the financial industry than to homeowners.[89] If the goal is to provide additional subsidies to low- and moderate-income homeowners, then a sizable tax credit for mortgage interest ought to do the trick. There is no reason to create a separate system of finance.

Put another way, a government guarantee of mortgage-backed securities is most directly a government subsidy to securitization and only very indirectly a subsidy of homeownership, and certainly not a subsidy that

---

89 See U.S. Departments of Treasury and Housing and Urban Development (2011).

progressives should support.[90] A structure of securitization that arises through the workings of the market might be a good way to allocate capital, but creating such a structure should not be the explicit goal of government policy. There may be a public interest in subsidizing home ownership, but there is no public interest in subsidizing mortgage securitization.

Universal retirement accounts

Another way in which to downsize the financial sector is to reduce the fees associated with its management of 401(k)s and other types of retirement savings accounts. These fees average more than 1.0 percent of the assets held in the accounts and in many cases exceed 1.5 percent. This is a huge drain on workers' savings, and the money paid out in fees comes directly out of the return in these accounts. Over 30 years, a 1.0 percent annual fee will reduce total returns by almost 25 percent. If the fees average 1.5 percent, the reduction will be 35 percent. In addition, the financial industry typically charges fees of around 10 percent for turning an accumulation into an annuity when a worker retires.[91]

These sorts of fees are pure waste. The fees for the federal employee Thrift Savings Plan average less than 0.15 percent of the money in the accounts. Well-run private plans, like Vanguard, keep their fees under 0.25 percent of account balances. If the average savings on a well-run plan is equal to 0.85 percent of the money in the funds, the cumulative savings over the course of decade could be more than $900 billion, as shown in **Figure 9-1**.

---

90 An analysis by Zandi and deRitis (2011) was widely held up as supporting a proposal for a new system of government guarantees. Their analysis estimated that a system of government guarantees would reduce the interest rate on 30-year fixed-rate mortgages by approximately 90 basis points (0.9 percentage points). This reduction in interest rates would be almost fully offset by an increase of approximately 8 percent in average home prices, leaving typical homeowners paying almost the same amount in their monthly mortgage payment. The analysis didn't show the full economic effects of this subsidy, but higher home prices would be expected to lead to more consumption through the wealth effect, implying reduced investment and slower growth.

91 This is in addition to the payment reductions associated with adverse selection, where insurers reduce annual payments under the assumption that people who buy annuities have longer life expectancies than the population as a whole.

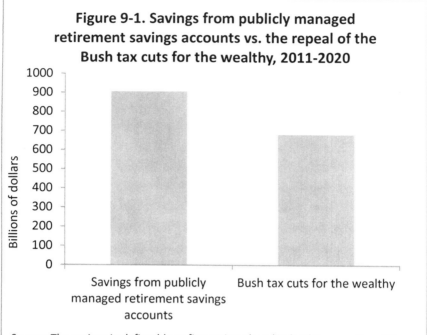

Figure 9-1. Savings from publicly managed retirement savings accounts vs. the repeal of the Bush tax cuts for the wealthy, 2011-2020

Source: The savings in defined-benefit pension plans (Federal Reserve Board Flow of Funds Accounts, Table L.118.c, Line 1) and savings in individual retirement accounts (Federal Reserve Board Flow of Funds Accounts, Table L.225.i, Line 1) are summed and then multiplied by0.85 percent. It is assumed that the accounts grow at the same rate as the economy. Bush tax cuts: Tax Policy Center (2010).

The government could offer a major service by making a version of the Thrift Savings Plan available as an option to every worker in the country.[92] This sort of voluntary system can also be put in place at the state level. Several states were close to implementing such a plan before the recession refocused policy makers' attention on other issues and made even the modest seed money needed for starting such a system unaffordable. (Once a plan is up and running, it would be fully paid for from fees charged to participants.)

---

92 It can also be made a default option in which a portion of workers' wages (e.g., 3 percent) is put into a savings fund every year, unless the worker opts out. If workers actively decided that they preferred to have the money to spend now or preferred some other savings vehicle, they need only decline the savings option (Baker and Rosnick, 2011). Several recent studies indicate that many workers will save more in situations where it is a default option. This proposal and others rely on this evidence.

There is widespread recognition across the political spectrum of the need to increase retirement savings,[93] and there is a great deal of evidence that a simple government-managed retirement account system can be more efficient than privately managed 401(k)s or IRAs. Why not give people the choice and let them decide for themselves?

The management of public pension funds

The financial industry makes a considerable sum from managing public pension funds, but there is good reason to question whether the industry is always acting in the best interests of the pension funds for which it works. For example, New York financier Steven Rattner, who also served a stint in the Obama administration overseeing the auto bailouts, agreed to pay a $10 million fine to end a suit charging that he made payoffs to gain oversight of $150 million in New York State pension funds.[94]

If investment fund managers are prepared to make payoffs to land contracts, then it is a safe bet that the state is not getting the best deal for managing its pension fund assets. This is a case where a little bit of transparency might go a long way. It should be possible to go to a pension fund website and see the exact terms of every management contract the fund signed, including the representatives of the fund who approved the contract. The pension fund should also show the returns, both before and after fees, of any money managed by private investors. Compiling and posting this information on the web every six months or each year should involve no more than a few hours of clerical work. Once it was posted anyone should be able to recognize any contracts that appear to be excessive or any returns that substantially underperform the market. Pension fund managers with a habit of directing investments to underperforming assets could be easily identified by any interested beneficiary or reporter.

Public postings may not completely prevent kickback schemes and sleazy deals, but the information should make such scams considerably more

---

93 For example, David John at the Heritage Foundation co-authored a paper advocating a government-managed voluntary system of defined-contribution pensions (Iwry and John, 2009).
94 See Popper (2010).

difficult to perpetuate. Furthermore, the cost is trivial, so there is no obvious reason for pension funds not to follow this practice.

Financial speculation tax

Another tool for downsizing the financial industry is a financial speculation tax of the sort the United Kingdom currently imposes on stock trades. This tax is a modest fee on trading stocks, bonds, options, futures, and other derivative instruments. It is both a revenue-raising measure and a way to discourage excessive speculation by raising its cost.

The sorts of fees involved with these trades would have almost no impact on normal financial activity. For example, the fee on stock trades in the United Kingdom is 0.5 percent on the purchase side of each trade. Since there has been a sharp reduction in trading costs over the last three decades as a result of computerization, a fee of this size would just raise trading costs back to their level of the mid-1980s, a time when the United States and the world had well-developed financial markets.

The potential revenue is substantial. The U.K. raises an amount that is close to 0.2 percent of its GDP (about 3 billion pounds per year, or the equivalent to about $30 billion a year in the United States) from just taxing stock trades. A tax applied to a broad range of assets should raise close to 1.0 percent of GDP, or about $150 billion a year in the United States and $1.8 trillion over the course of a decade. These sums dwarf the revenue from eliminating the Bush tax cuts for the wealthy (**Figure 9-2**).

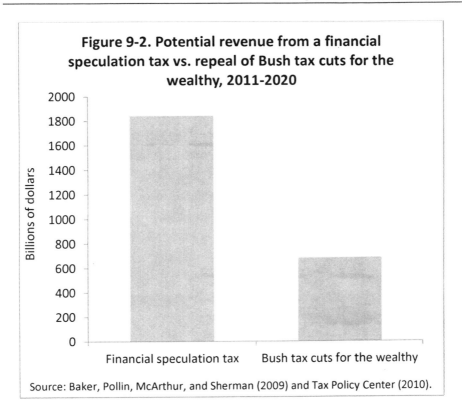

Figure 9-2. Potential revenue from a financial speculation tax vs. repeal of Bush tax cuts for the wealthy, 2011-2020

Source: Baker, Pollin, McArthur, and Sherman (2009) and Tax Policy Center (2010).

This money would come almost entirely at the expense of the financial industry as opposed to actors in the productive economy. Several studies have shown that trading is very responsive to changes in costs, which means that if a tax raised costs, the volume of trading would fall sharply. In other words, the higher cost per trade (including the tax) would be offset for most people by a reduced volume of trading. For example, investors with $100,000 in a 401(k) who made $20,000 in trades every year before the imposition of a tax might reduce the volume of their trading to $10,000 a year after the tax. If the tax doubled the cost of the trade, then they would be spending no more on trading after the tax was imposed than they did before.

The only loser in this story is the financial industry. Money that had been going to the industry in fees would instead be collected by the government in taxes. The end result will be a smaller, more efficient financial industry, exactly what any good economist should want.

While a financial speculation tax would most likely have to be implemented at the national level, states could implement a financial activities tax (FAT) along the lines recommended by the IMF.[95] A FAT would be, in effect, a type of sales tax on financial activity of all sorts, most of which now goes largely untaxed. A 5 percent tax imposed on all financial-sector activity could raise more than $115 billion a year. This tax would not be as well-targeted on wasteful speculative trades as a transactions-based speculation tax, but its ease of implementation means that a progressive legislature in any state could tap a major new source of revenue at the expense of the financial sector. It is unfortunate that the tax will also hit ordinary transactions by average people, but it's hard to see why it is okay (in many states) to tax food but not to tax checking account fees or credit card penalties.

Corporate governance, the much-overlooked cesspool

It is remarkable that conservatives, who are inherently suspicious of governmental institutions, tend to pay little attention to the structure of corporate governance. Just as governments at all levels offer the opportunity for corruption, so do corporations. The big difference is that corporate managers – unlike their counterparts in government – operate largely in secret, control many of the rules under which they are re-elected, and make payoffs (in the form of directors' fees) to the people who determine their salaries.

Former Illinois Governor Rod Blagojevich gained national notoriety over the tape recordings of his discussion of plans to sell the Senate seat vacated by Barack Obama after he was elected president. The chief executive officers running most major companies can be viewed as little Blagojeviches, but unlike the governor they don't have to go through the trouble of breaking the law to get more money into their pockets.

In most corporations, CEOs play a large role in selecting the board that determines their pay. If they decide they want more compensation, whether in straight pay or in the form of an increased bonus or pension, they are likely to have a receptive audience. After all, board members are typically

---

95 IMF (2010).

paid several hundred thousand dollars a year for attending four to eight meetings, and they will naturally be grateful to the person who gave them this plum job and who could take it away from them if they prove uncooperative. The CEOs keep getting higher pay, the board members get to pocket $200,000, $300,000, or $400,000 a year, and everyone is happy.

Where do the stockholders fit into this picture? It's difficult for ordinary stockholders to organize, just as it is difficult for average voters to unite to ensure that their elected officials act in their interest. In addition to facing the same problems in organizing as voters face in local, state, or national elections, shareholders also must deal with the fact that corporate managers can rig the election rules to make it more difficult for shareholders to overturn management decisions.

For example, it is standard practice to treat uncast proxy votes as votes cast in support of management's position. This rule can make it all but impossible to pass a shareholder resolution on an issue like cutting the pay of top management. Also, if top management can count on the support of one or two major shareholders, who might be mutual fund managers, then it will be almost impossible for shareholders to overrule decisions on executive compensation or anything else.

Shareholders can always just sell their shares, and undoubtedly this is a wise move if corruption in a company gets out of hand. But it rarely gets out of hand, relatively speaking. In major corporations annual profits can easily reach $10 billion a year. If the CEO and top management overpay themselves by $200 million a year, their greed might translate into just 2 to 3 percent of corporate profits. Just as with government waste, this may be a big sum to the individuals directly involved, but it generally doesn't make much difference to the bottom line. In both cases, it is usually more difficult to weed out the waste than it is worth, which means that managers are likely to get away with excessive pay under the current system.

This discussion is especially relevant to the financial sector because there is nowhere else in the economy where pay has diverged so sharply from performance for shareholders. The top executives of companies like Lehman Brothers, Fannie Mae, and Freddie Mac received huge paychecks based on short-term profits, which encouraged them to take outsized risks that, in effect, were one-sided bets. Every year that the bets paid off allowed the

CEOs and other top managers to put huge sums in their pockets. But if the bets went bad the CEOs could simply walk away with their prior earnings, and perhaps bonuses and a severance. After the executives drove their companies to bankruptcy, shareholders were left with little or nothing while the CEOs walked away with fortunes.[96]

It is not difficult to structure contracts so that incentives are aligned more closely with the long-term performance of the stock and so that top management doesn't do well unless the shareholders do well. (We may be concerned about corporate stakeholders other than shareholders as well, but it would be a big step forward to have a pay structure that at least protected shareholders.) But the boards that set pay are working for the CEOs, not the shareholders, and so outsized pay packages are likely to persist unless there are major changes in the rules of corporate governance.[97]

The outlandish CEO pay packages of today are a relatively new development. While CEOs have always been well paid, the ratio of executive compensation to the average worker's pay was in the range of 25 or 30 to 1 as recently as the 1970s, which would put CEO compensation in the area of $1.5-$2.0 million. By contrast, multiples of 200 or 300 to 1 are the norm today. One would be hard-pressed to argue that CEOs as a group are doing a better job now than in the 1950s and 1960s, when the country enjoyed its most rapid rate of productivity growth.

Moreover, CEO pay in the United States is hugely out of line with CEO pay in the rest of the world. The top executives of big companies like Volkswagen, Toyota, and Sony are likely to have pay packages in the low millions, not the tens of millions and certainly not hundreds of millions, like their counterparts in the United States. This level of compensation has not prevented these companies from finding executives who have been able to run the business profitably. The best guess to explain the huge difference in CEO

---

96 Remarkably, many of these CEOs continue to be sought-after executives. Daniel Mudd and Richard Fuld, the CEOs who, respectively, led Fannie Mae and Lehman into bankruptcy, both are again employed in high-paying jobs in finance.

97 The "say on pay" provision of the Dodd-Frank financial reform bill requires companies to have nonbinding shareholder votes on executive compensation packages. This is a step forward that will at least call greater attention to outlandish pay packages, but by itself is likely to have little effect on CEO pay.

compensation between the United States and other wealthy countries is that it is attributable primarily to the laws and norms of corporate governance, not the inherent workings of the market.

As discussed in Chapter 8, we should welcome other opportunities to find lower-cost top management. CEOs take this approach when they look for the lowest-cost workers, and the rest of us ought to take the same approach when it comes to top management.

We should also use every lever at our disposal, such as the power of pension funds, socially responsible investment funds, or socially minded individual investors to bring CEO pay back in line with international standards. This activism is not really a great leap in principle. CEOs are ripping off their companies. Why not use the market to overcome a problem of bad governance?

Chapter 10

Government-Granted Monopolies Are Not Small Government

One of the main problems facing progressives is that they do not control the terms of the debate. Nowhere is this more true than in the case of patents and copyrights. These are both government-granted monopolies and forms of interference in a free market. Yet these policies, under the guise of "intellectual property," are treated as a natural part of the market. Enforcing them is treated as supporting the free market, whereas opposing them is viewed as government intervention.

Huge amounts of money are stake with these claims to property. We spend close to $300 billion a year on prescription drugs that would sell for around $30 billion in a competitive market. This difference of $270 billion a year is more than five times as large as the annual cost of President Bush's tax cuts for the wealthiest 2 percent of the population. Computer software sales are more than $80 billion a year.[98] Sales of recorded music, movies, and video material easily come to more than $20 billion a year. Textbook sales alone

---

98 This figure is derived from the industry's claim that the value that it assigns to "pirated" software was $59 billion in 2010 and that this was equal to 42 percent of total software shipments; see Business Software Alliance (2011).

total over $9 billion a year.[99] Video games account for another $25 billion in annual sales.[100] The patents and copyrights that protect these revenues are public policies, not individual rights. Intellectual property is actually mentioned in the Constitution, though it is not a right guaranteed to individuals by the Bill of Rights. The ability to convey monopolies for limited periods of time, like patents and copyrights, is one of the powers explicitly delegated to Congress, like the power to tax.

Furthermore, the power to grant patent and copyright protection is tied to a specific purpose: "to promote the progress of science and useful arts." The language implies no individual right: the Constitution simply gives Congress the authority to create patent and copyright monopolies as a way to promote innovation and creative work. It does not require Congress to create these monopolies any more than it requires Congress to tax people. The policy question that needs to be addressed is whether patents and copyrights are the most effective mechanism for promoting innovation and creative work.

The case of drug patents

The serious issues that surround the efficacy of patents as a tool to promote innovation in a modern economy are especially striking in the context of drug patents.[101] Patents tend to have a more pernicious impact in the case of prescription drugs than in most other sectors of the economy, for two reasons.

First, drugs are a standalone consumer product, rather than an innovation or a feature for which a company can negotiate with the patent owner to allow for its efficient use. For example, an auto manufacturer might negotiate for the use of a patented technology in the production of its cars. The efficient outcome is that the marginal cost of the patent is zero. In other

---

99 Milliot (2010).

100 Newzoo (2011).

101 There is a whole industry of "patent trolls," individuals or firms that buy up patents with the hope of finding a major innovation that is arguably derivative of the patent in question. The profit comes from filing a patent infringement suit. The troll just needs to be able to make a plausible case so that it can threaten the company with the possibility of an expensive legal suit and/or an injunction denying the company the use of the technology. This is generally sufficient to force a settlement even if the case for actual infringement is weak.

words, the car manufacturer can either buy the patent outright or license it for a specific period of time, but its cost for using the patent on an additional car is zero. This is not possible with drugs, as the patented product is sold directly to patients.

The other major difference is that there is enormous asymmetry in knowledge about the product. The drug company will know much more about the effectiveness and safety of a drug than will the patient or even a well-informed doctor. The company has access to test results that are not in the public domain. This means that it is almost impossible to make a fully informed decision about the use of a particular drug.

It also matters that drugs involve people's health or even their lives. Most people will pay almost any price to protect their life or the life of a loved one. Giving the drug companies' monopoly control over potentially life-saving drugs is like allowing firefighters to negotiate their pay package with the homeowner when the house is on fire. Needless to say, firefighters would be very well paid under these circumstances, and drug companies raise enormous revenue under the patent system.

The importance of prescription drugs to our lives and health belies the fact that they are cheap. Few could not be profitably manufactured and distributed for less than $10 per prescription. The reason that we face moral dilemmas about paying $80,000 a year for a drug that may extend the life of an 80-year-old cancer patient by a few years is that we give drug companies patent monopolies that allow them to charge $80,000 a year. If the drugs were sold in a free market, we could avoid the dilemma and pay about $200 a year, making this a simple choice.

Of course, the research and testing necessary to bring a drug to market has enormous costs. But this expenditure has already been made when the drug comes on the market. The key goal of progressive policy should be to separate the payment for the research from the payment for the drug. If the payment for the research is made independent of the payment for the drug, then all drugs can be sold in a free market without patent monopolies, just as generic drugs are sold today.

The two main alternatives for financing research apart from the patent system are a prize system and direct public funding. Both would involve an expansion of public funding for biomedical research.[102] Currently, the federal government spends $30 billion a year on biomedical research through the National Institutes of Health. For an additional $30 billion to $80 billion it could replace the research currently funded through the patent system. Even taking the higher figure, the government would soon recoup this cost through savings on drug expenses in Medicare, Medicaid, and other public health programs.

A prize system would effectively buy out patents from drug companies, with the price determined based on some measure of a new drug's effectiveness and importance. After buying the patent, the government would place it in the public domain, where any manufacturer could use it.

A system of direct public funding would pay for research in advance. Companies would contract with a government agency, for example, a much-expanded version of the National Institutes of Health. A limited number would receive large long-term contracts (e.g., lasting 10-12 years) to support research into specified areas. As the end of the contract period approached, companies could reapply for a contract based on their track record of achievement.

All the results, both preclinical and clinical, would be public, a transparency that should allow researchers to make informed assessments of the relative efficacy of different drugs and determine if some drugs are better for specific groups of individuals.[103] The patents would be in the public domain, and so the drugs developed through this system would be sold at generic prices.

Getting from the current system of patent monopolies to a system of free-market drugs will be a Herculean task. The pharmaceutical industry is enormously powerful, and it can be expected to use all its resources to prevent any major changes to the patent system. In addition, overhauling the way the country finances prescription drug research will undoubtedly sound scary to

---

102 These mechanisms are described more fully in Baker (2004).

103 Patients often have multiple ailments, so it would be important to know if a particular heart medication was likely to have bad effects for people who are being treated for arthritis. It is also likely that drugs might differ in effectiveness based on characteristics like sex, age, and weight. Typically drug companies will not provide the information necessary to make these sorts of assessments.

many people.

An intermediate step that might make the shift less scary and certainly make it less expensive would be to have public funding for the clinical testing of drugs, which, according to the industry, accounts for close to 60 percent of research costs, while leaving the preclinical research supported by patents. In this scenario, patents would be bought out for testing, with the results placed in the public domain. This arrangement would put an end to the worst marketing abuses by the drug industry and still allow drugs to be sold at their free-market price.

Potential allies among industry groups for this sort of shift include the small innovative drug companies that tend not to do well in the current system. Generally, these companies race to find a valuable patent before they run out of funding, with most not succeeding.

Another potential ally is insurers who want to save money on drug costs, but a large-scale restructuring of a major health care sector might hit too close to home for their comfort. In principle, even the large pharmaceutical companies could be allies, since there is no reason that they could not profit as much under either a prize system or a system of direct funding as under a patent system.

The real expertise of the major pharmaceutical manufacturers at present is their marketing, not their innovation. They typically buy many of the patents for the drugs they market from smaller startups. For this reason, a system that effectively eliminated the huge profits from the marketing of drugs that can be sold at monopolistic prices would undermine the companies' whole way of doing business. As a result, the big pharmaceutical companies can be expected to strongly oppose any major reform of the patent system.

But this is a case where the market can be used to undermine the industry's position. A substantial number of drugs currently flow into the United States from Canada and other countries who, rather than grant pharmaceutical companies unrestricted monopolies, instead set limits on the extent to which drug companies can exploit their patent monopolies. As a result, drug prices in Canada are 30 to 60 percent less than prices in the United States.

Progressives should promote this trade wherever possible. For example, by organizing bus trips from neighboring states into Canada to allow people to buy low-cost drugs, or by supporting efforts by state and local governments to fight federal restrictions on their ability to buy cheaper drugs from other countries for their workers' health care plans, their state Medicaid programs, and their residents more generally.

Progressives should also actively oppose conditions in trade agreements that force other countries to impose U.S.-type patent rules. Patent restrictions could be a life-or-death matter for tens of millions of people in the developing world who may be able to afford drugs at their market price now but will find the patent-protected price impossibly expensive. In addition, by extending the reach of U.S.-type patent rules, these trade agreements eliminate potential sources of low-cost drugs for people in the United States.

It is important to understand what is at stake here. The pharmaceutical industry wants government-imposed monopolies to allow it to make huge profits. The rest of us want free markets. The amount of money involved in this sector dwarfs the amount at stake in most government programs. When conservatives talk about $10 billion or $20 billion a year for child care or family assistance programs, we should turn the discussion to the drug industry which is costing $270 billion a year in higher payments for its patent-protected drugs. It is the pharmaceutical industry that wants big government and wants a powerful state that will arrest competitors who undercut its monopoly prices. Progressives should want a free market.

Copyright is big government in your bedroom, not the free market

Copyrights for books, recorded music, movies, video games, software, and other items present the same sort of issue as patent protection for prescription drugs. Items that would essentially be available at zero cost in a free market can instead command high prices because the government grants copyright monopolies. While the consequences of copyright protection are not as pernicious, – in the sense that people's lives generally do not depend on access to copyrighted material, – the cost to the public of copyright protection is enormous. Including software, the public spends more than $100 billion a year for items that would be available at much lower or even zero cost in a free market.

In addition to the direct cost in the form of above-market prices, copyright enforcement in the Internet age also incurs enormous costs. And the government has eagerly assisted the publishing, entertainment, and software industries in their efforts to protect and extend their monopolies.

Many of the measures taken are absurd. For example, the government has repeatedly extended the period of copyright (now 95 years after the death of the author) and applied the extensions retroactively. This is bizarre: the purpose of copyright monopolies is to provide incentives for creative work, and it is impossible to provide incentives retroactively. These retroactive extensions are sometimes dubbed the "Mickey Mouse Law," since Disney, hoping to keep its copyright on Mickey Mouse in force further into the future, was a major proponent of the extensions.

Enforcement actions have involved police breaking into dorm rooms and high school kids' bedrooms in search of computers allegedly used to download copyrighted material without authorization. Police arrested a Russian computer scientist after an academic talk in Denver for work he had done on breaking encryption codes in Russia (where it was completely legal). Copying devices have been banned from the market because they did not have adequate safeguards to protect copyrighted material. In one civil prosecution, a young mother in Minnesota was fined hundreds of thousands of dollars for using her computer to share two dozen copyrighted songs. The Recording Industry Association of America has even developed propaganda courses on the evils of unauthorized reproductions (a.k.a. pirated copyrighted material).

This effort to enforce copyright is both very big government and very wasteful. No genuine "small government conservative" would support this sort of extraordinary intervention in the market and interference with people's lives. Creative workers need to be compensated for their work, but copyright is an inefficient mechanism for accomplishing this goal. There are alternative mechanisms for supporting creative work, several of which are already in existence.

The most important alternative mechanism is probably the university system, in which faculty are expected to publish in their areas of expertise in addition to teaching. The work supported in this way is mostly designed for professional audiences, but a substantial body of work produced by university faculty is intended for general audiences. In addition to universities, private foundations support a large amount of creative work in writing, music, and the arts more generally. In the United States, the federal government supports a substantial amount of creative work through the National Endowment for the Arts and the National Endowment for the Humanities, and indirectly through the Corporation for Public Broadcasting. State and local governments also provide limited support. Of course, in most other wealthy countries, the government provides considerably more support for creative work.

As it stands, the amount of work supported through mechanisms other than copyright is almost certainly less than what society would desire, which suggests the need to expand the existing mechanisms and/or create new ones. In the case of the United States, expanding the government's role is likely to meet considerable resistance, in part because people may object to having the government fund work they dislike and also because they may not like the idea of the government having a big hand in determining what creative work gets support.

It is not difficult to get around this problem. One way would be an "artistic freedom voucher," a refundable tax credit for a specific amount (e.g., $100) that individuals could contribute to whatever creative worker/organization they choose. [104] The condition of getting this money would be that the recipient individuals/organizations would not be eligible to receive copyrights for some period of time (e.g., three years) after receiving the money. All the work they produced would be in the public domain so that it could be reproduced and circulated around the world.

One benefit of this structure is its low enforcement costs. Artists who had received voucher money and then tried to violate the rules and get a copyright would find their copyright unenforceable. Anyone would have the right to freely reproduce the material as though the copyright did not exist.

This mechanism is not very different from the current tax deduction for charitable organizations. As it stands, wealthy individuals can make large charitable contributions that are subsidized by the government through the tax deduction. If people in the top tax bracket give $10 million to their local symphony, the government effectively subsidizes this contribution by reducing their tax liability by $3,600,000.

---

104 This mechanism is outlined more fully in Baker (2003).

In the case of the artistic freedom vouchers, the whole payment would come from the government, rather than just a fraction, but the sums involved would be much smaller. Instead of giving millions of dollars in subsidies to a small number of individuals, the system would give a modest subsidy to hundreds of millions of individuals. There would inevitably be some amount of gaming and fraud, as there is with the charitable deduction, but it would likely be limited, as the potential gains would be small relative to the opportunities that already exist with the charitable deduction.[105]

The advantage of an artistic freedom voucher system is that it preserves individuals' choice in determining what creative work that they wish to support. It separates the decision to buy material from the decision to support a specific type of creative work. Presumably people will mostly support the type of work they actually enjoy, but they would have the option of supporting one type of work even if they don't enjoy it themselves. For example, they might support classical music even if they listen only to rock music. The important point is that it would be a matter of individual choice, not a decision made by a government agency.

The obstacles to moving from the copyright world we have today to the artistic freedom voucher world described above are enormous, but there are important market forces pushing in this direction as well as powerful potential allies.

The opponents of this sort of transformation include the entertainment industry, a large, politically powerful industry that will do everything possible to preserve and extend its copyright monopolies. The entertainment industry is also influential among many progressive politicians because it is one of the few pockets of wealth that have been a reliable source of support in political campaigns. The software and publishing industries are also quite powerful. In the latter case, the fact that newspapers weigh in on political campaigns is also likely to be a deterrent to elected officials who want

---

105 Simple restrictions could go far toward eliminating some of the obvious opportunities for small-scale fraud. For example, requiring that an individual or organization get some minimal amount (e.g., $2,500) would prevent any sort of simple trade-off scheme in which individuals exchanged their vouchers among themselves. Arranging for 25 people to give their vouchers to one person or organization in a kickback scheme might be possible, but it would involve considerable effort and risk for limited gain.

to weaken copyright protections or propose alternatives.

As with patent monopolies, the market is a powerful force working against copyright monopolies. While the industry groups can be expected to continually invent new locks and search mechanisms to prevent the reproduction of copyrighted material and to trace its transmission path, innovative software engineers will be equally energetic in designing ways to crack locks and avoid detection.

Progressives should be on the side of the free flow of material, which means opposing repressive legislation that increases penalties for reproducing and circulating copyrighted pieces. It also means opposing efforts to promote the spread and extension of copyright protection, such as those in trade agreements that force U.S. trading partners to impose stronger copyright laws. (This is the sort of issue that could lead to a productive trade agreement with China's government. We could tell them they can apply their own laws to Microsoft's software and Disney's movies, and they could agree to raise the value of the yuan against the dollar.) Progressives should also oppose the use of propaganda courses in schools and universities that tout the virtues of copyrights.

In addition, progressives should support in every way possible the creation and circulation of free music, movies, software, and other creative material. This support can take a variety of forms. A vast body of material is already available on the web that is not subject to restrictive copyrights. It includes work that was always in the public domain, work that has fallen into the public domain because of the expiration of copyrights, and work that is subject to Creative Commons copyright. The latter is a less-exclusive form of copyright that can allow for free distribution of material.[106] The promotion of this material can further acclimate the public to work that is not protected by copyright.

Private foundations can also be sources of support for non-copyright-protected material. As part of an economic development strategy, state and

---

106 This book is subject to a Creative Commons copyright that allows for its free reproduction. The one exclusion is that the copyright requires the author's permission to publish the material in an altered form. The purpose of this restriction is to prevent the misrepresentation of material in this book. Libel law also provides protection against misrepresentation, but the copyright restrictions are more easily enforced.

local governments could create artistic freedom voucher systems involving some modest amount per resident, like the federal programs described above. However, a condition of receiving money could be that the musician, writer, singer, or other creative workers physically live within the state or city for at least eight months a year, in addition to forgoing a copyright. Musicians and other creative workers living in a state or city for eight months a year would almost certainly plan to perform there or in other ways practice their work, both as a way of earning money and making themselves more popular among the residents and thereby better positioned to get voucher money.

A state or city setting up this sort of system could become a cultural mecca, where hundreds of musicians performed their music every night and theaters produced original plays. Writers could have workshops to train aspiring writers, and all manner of creative workers could receive lessons in their areas of specialization. A large inflow of visitors would take advantage of these offerings. For depressed areas with a good housing stock and scenic environment, this could be a promising development path.

It would be easier for a state or local government to follow this path if it received a grant from a foundation to pick up part of the expense. For example, an Albany-size city of 100,000 could have $10 million to support artistic freedom vouchers if it received a $5 million grant and could come up with $5 million itself. The prospect of garnering some portion of this money could bring a large number of creative workers to the city from surrounding areas. This sum would be sufficient to provide $25,000 to 400 creative workers, a substantial subsidy to the living standards of many workers struggling to get by.

Cities and states can explicitly promote free material in the textbooks they use in schools at all levels. A number of high school and college textbooks are already available for free downloads without copyright protection.[107] In many cases these books are perfectly adequate substitutes for expensive copyrighted textbooks. State and local governments could also contract with academics to write textbooks that will be available freely to their students

---

107 Hundreds of textbooks available for free download can be found at Open Education
    Resources Commons: http://www.oercommons.org/.

online. These will almost certainly cost far less than having students buy textbooks individually through the copyright system, especially if the process can be coordinated among many governments. Several states have already gone this route.

As a basic principle, free material will drive out copyrighted material. If people have access to quality work for which they don't have to pay, why should they pay for copyrighted material? The model here is Wikipedia, which offers entries that are every bit as accurate as those available from traditional encyclopedias on a far wider range of topics. As a result, it has virtually eliminated the market for traditional encyclopedias.

A challenge will be to find mechanisms for ensuring that creative workers are paid decent wages. However, few creative workers are able to earn decent livelihoods under the copyright system, so we don't have a model that works now. We surely can do better.

The push for material unprotected by copyright should extend to software as well. Open and ideally free software is preferable to protected software. In this philosophy Google and Linux (originally GNU/Linux, in recognition of its roots in the free software movement) are preferable to Microsoft and Apple. Computers and other devices with freely available software should cost less. And any system that is constantly improved by tens of thousands of people will be far better than a system designed in the closed confines of a corporate production process. (Is there anyone anywhere who would be using a Microsoft *anything* if the company had not used its market power to gain a dominant position in software?)

The move to a non-copyright-protected world should lead us to better and more widely available creative material and software, and put an end to some of the concentrations of wealth created by the copyright system. Microsoft could be the new Commodore, Disney could truly be a Mickey Mouse outfit, and Rupert Murdoch could retire as a less-wealthy patron of right-wing causes.

Chapter 11

Follow the Money:
The Guiding Light for a Progressive Strategy

In the fall of 2007, as the collapse of the housing bubble was about to crash the economy, the biggest economic concern under debate in Congress was a budget deficit that at the time was equal to 1.2 percent of GDP, or roughly $180 billion in the 2011 economy.

Then, as now, the political debate over economic policy was a sideshow to the real economic issues that most affected people's lives. The obsession over a relatively small budget deficit helped to drown out warnings about an economic tsunami that would soon throw more than eight million people out of work, cause millions to lose their homes, and cost the country more than $4 trillion in lost output. The effects of this collapse will have added trillions of dollars to the national debt when all is said and done.

But no one in a leadership position in Washington wanted to talk about the housing bubble in 2007. There was a budget deficit to worry about. Obsessing about budget issues while ignoring fundamental economic issues led to a disaster with consequences for the budget that were far worse than any budget hawk could have feared in 2007. If the budget hawks really cared about the deficit and debt, they should have focused their efforts on the economy and ignored the budget, rather than the other way around.

Progressives have been similarly shortsighted by misdirecting their attention to the narrow realm of tax and transfer policy while largely ignoring far more important policies that determine the distribution of before-tax income. As a result, conservatives have gained control of the mechanisms that distribute income and used tax and transfer policy as a sideshow to divert public attention.

The arithmetic on this story is straightforward. Federal government spending averages roughly 20 percent of GDP. Adding in state and local government spending gets us a bit over 30 percent. This means that all levels of government spending account for less than one-third of the economy. If this is the exclusive realm for political debate, and we ignore the way in which the government structures the larger economy, then we have given up two-thirds of the game.

Even worse, this approach leaves progressives much less well-situated to contest the portion of income that is controlled by the government for both political and economic reasons.

Politically, the idea of taking money from the people who have lots of it and giving it to those who have not earned much is always going to be problematic, especially in the United States. The idea of government redistribution does not sell well.

It also poses economic problems. Conservatives' complaints about the economic distortions created by high taxes have some basis in reality, even if they are often hugely overstated. Progressives should steer clear of the potential for being seen as having an agenda that means slower growth and less job creation.

Shifting attention to before-tax issues of income means talking about the big policy items, most importantly the Fed and the dollar, that have the greatest impact on economic outcomes. Though the chance of achieving major policy changes in these areas in the near future is slim, the public should at least understand the importance of the Fed and the value of the dollar in determining economic outcomes. Continuing to pursue low-inflation and high-dollar policies will leave tens of millions of people unemployed or underemployed, and the public should understand that this path is a choice made by those in power.

It is also important to change the orientation of progressive thinking and rhetoric both to achieve success politically and to get better policy outcomes even on less consequential issues. A recent debate on restricting the government-subsidized student loans available to low- and middle-income students to pay tuition at for-profit colleges provides an excellent case in point. The right managed to turn this argument on its head, successfully portraying itself as the protector of a free market and the Obama administration and Democrats in Congress as supporters of increased government regulation.

Proponents of restricting the availability of these loans argued that many students use the loans at schools where they often do not complete a degree or from which they fail to land a job even with a degree. This outcome leaves the students with large debts and little ability to repay them, and leaves the government on the hook since it guarantees the loans.

The intention of the new regulations was to ensure that students used the loans only at schools that provide their graduates with reasonable prospects for "gainful employment" (determined by graduates' debt-to-income ratios and loan repayment rates). This was a regulation of the loan program to prevent abuse and to ensure that the money was doing what was intended: helping low- and middle-income students get the education and skills they need to get a good job.

What position do you think an advocate of free markets would take in this debate? Obviously, a true free-marketer would eliminate the program altogether. It's a subsidy that interferes in the education market.

But for-profit colleges wanted and needed the subsidy (as up to 90 percent of their revenue comes from taxpayer-provided student loans and grants), and so in true conservative fashion they turned the debate into a battle between those who favored a "free market" (them) and those who wanted increased government regulation. The industry argued that it would be strangled and many colleges would be put out of business by the new regulations.

It is almost impossible to exaggerate the absurdity of this position. Nothing being proposed would prevent the schools from doing whatever they wanted or prevent any students from choosing to attend any school they wanted. The debate was over the limitations applied to a government aid program. The for-profit college industry essentially opposed clamping down on fraud (bogus colleges); it wanted the freedom to rip off students and taxpayers and did not want the government to get in the way.

We can view this through another example. New York City Mayor Michael Bloomberg and others have advocated that food stamp recipients be prohibited from using food stamps on soda and sugary drinks. Regardless of the merits of this policy, there is little doubt that it is being proposed as a limitation on food stamp recipients and what they can do with this government benefit.

While Mayor Bloomberg proposed this as a simple exclusion of certain items from the list of products that could be purchased with food stamps, it would almost certainly lead to a situation where there would be a substantial number of products that fell into a grey area (for example sweetened ice tea). This in turn would likely mean establishing standards that the industry would have to show that they met in order to avoid being excluded from the program. The requirement for meeting some set of nutritional standards would be comparable to the record-keeping requirements that the for-profit college industry claimed would be onerous. In other words, prohibiting food stamp beneficiaries from buying soft drinks with their food stamps would impose requirements on the food industry, just as restricting the use of student loans imposes requirements on the for-profit college industry.

In this event, would the makers of soft drinks manage to pitch their objections as a complaint about intrusive government regulation interfering with the free market? Would the proponents of increasing the restrictions on the use of food stamps be labeled as advocates of stronger government regulation? That seems unlikely but that is exactly what happened in the effort to prevent abuses of the student loan system.

The position of the for-profit colleges had nothing to do with the free market. Yet the progressives pushing for tighter regulation and accountability ceded ground, agreeing to a four-year-long "three strikes and you're out" examination before a school could lose eligibility for the government giveaway. "We believe that very few programs will be forcibly closed by our standards," Secretary of Education Arne Duncan said. "We want to give people a chance to reform. As a country, we need this sector to succeed. This is not about 'gotcha.'"[108] Of course, the issue is not "gotcha;" the issue is a pattern of abuses that borders on criminal fraud, and the secretary of education essentially committed the department to not taking them seriously.

It is interesting to ask whether the outcome of the student loan fight would have been different if the proponents of the new regulations had insisted on characterizing them as an effort to limit waste in a government program for low- and moderate-income people, which is in fact what the regulations were.

The caricature of conservatives as anti-government and progressives as pro-government makes arguments in support of huge government programs like Social Security and Medicare confusing and difficult. At least in the case of these two massive social insurance programs, the vast majority of the public – regardless of political affiliation – supports their purpose of providing necessary protections to the elderly and disabled. And, for this reason, conservatives who want to dismantle these programs almost never argue that we don't need a Social Security or Medicare-type system; they argue that their privatized system will be better than the current government-run system. (In nearly 20 years of policy debates in Washington and around the country I don't believe that I have confronted a conservative who advocated simply eliminating these programs.)

In this instance, we are debating not values but whether privatized systems can provide the protections – which both sides seem to agree are desirable – more efficiently. And the evidence is overwhelming that privatization adds unnecessary costs to providing retirement income security or health care. Part of the cost is the profits that private firms extract, but much of the increase is associated with the inefficiency of a decentralized system as opposed to a single centralized system.

In selecting most goods and services, we value choice, but there is not much value to individual choice in the way we receive our core retirement income. People want to know the money will be there – end of story. Marketing and creating 20 different flavors of the same product simply makes providing a secure retirement income more expensive.

Extensive experience with privatized systems throughout Latin America and elsewhere in the developing world, as well as in some wealthy

---

108 Lewin (2011).

countries like the United Kingdom, bears this out. We also have the private retirement system in the United States if we need evidence that the debate over privatizing Social Security is a debate over whether workers want to see their retirement income reduced so that the financial industry can have more money. The only values question here is whether it is better for workers to keep their money or for the financial industry to have it.

The same story applies to efforts to privatize Medicare. The Congressional Budget Office's analysis of the Republican Party's voucher plan (which the House of Representatives approved) projected that the plan would raise the cost of buying Medicare-equivalent policies by $34 trillion over Medicare's 75-year planning period.[109] The issue in this case is simply whether retired workers want to have $34 trillion pulled out of their pockets and handed to the insurance and health care industries.

Framing this as a debate over values is a distraction. The right claims its goal is "to get government off our backs," but it would merely replace one method of providing retirement security and health care with another. It says its way of providing these services is better, but the evidence shows that's not the case. And that, pure and simple, is why the right makes this a values debate.

Bringing back the market

The cases of Social Security and Medicare are great examples of how the logic of the market leads to progressive outcomes. In these cases a simple centralized system is more efficient than a decentralized, privatized system. There is no need to contrast the logic of the government and the logic of the market: if we want efficient programs, we want ones that look like Social Security and Medicare.

In the same vein, we can structure the market more generally to produce progressive outcomes. The enormous growth of inequality over the last three decades did not come about as the result of the natural workings of the market; it came about through conscious design. The job of progressives is to point this out in every venue and in every way we can. It is not by luck,

---

109 Rosnick and Baker (2011a).

talent, and hard work that the rich are getting so much richer. It is by rigging the rules of the game.

From a political perspective it is much better to say that the progressive agenda is about setting fair rules for the market. The argument that highly paid professionals should face the same international competition as factory workers is a compelling one, and more arresting than the argument that we should redistribute money from the winners to the losers.

Since public debate is so badly misinformed on almost all economic issues, most people will be hearing these arguments for the first time. Few realize that an agency of the government, the Federal Reserve Board, actively throws people out of work to fight inflation. Few know that the loss of manufacturing jobs and the downward pressure on the wages of manufacturing workers are not accidental outcomes of trade agreements but rather the whole basis for them. (The enigma of trade is that it can make a whole country richer and yet most of its people poorer.) And hardly anyone understands that a higher-valued dollar intensifies the hurtful effect of trade by putting further downward pressure on the wages of workers subject to international competition.

Our Federal Reserve policy, trade policy, and dollar policy redistribute income upward from the less advantaged to those who disproportionately control the nation's wealth and political power. Each policy is designed for this outcome. Knowing this economic reality is not the same as changing it, but it is an important first step.

Progressives have to start playing hardball. The right is not just trying to win elections; it is working to destroy the basis of progressive opposition. Breaking private-sector unions in the 1980s was not just about getting lower-cost labor; it was also a deliberate effort to undermine one of the pillars of progressive politics in the United States. Recent efforts at the state and federal levels to weaken public sector unions are not about saving money for the government; they are a deliberate effort to destroy the strongest remaining segment of the labor movement.

Progressives must think the same way. When a Medicare patient has $50,000 to put in her pocket after receiving a heart bypass operation in Singapore rather than Topeka (remember that the government also saves $50,000), she is a walking advertisement for the waste and inefficiency of the

U.S. health care system. Every person who takes advantage of these health care savings will make a mockery of the politicians from both parties who have the gall to say the U.S. health care system is the best in the world.

When we convince a state or local government to contract out its architectural or engineering design tasks to lower-cost firms in India or Brazil, to purchase open-source software and textbooks for its students, and to fill its Medicaid prescriptions through low-cost Canadian suppliers, we un-rig the protections set up for highly paid professionals, copyright holders, and pharmaceutical firms and demonstrate that the market can save ordinary people money.

Success will build on success, just as it has for the right. If a progressive state gets its unemployment rate down to 4 percent through work sharing, or cuts its Medicaid spending by 30 percent by using medical trade and foreign pharmaceuticals, others will follow.

These innovations will also have a cumulative effect that amplifies their impact. If work sharing brings the unemployment rate in a state down to 4 percent, then ordinary workers in that state will be far more likely to see wage increases. They also may feel more empowered to unionize, since the threat of job loss has much less consequence in a situation where it is relatively easy to find another job.

Moreover, the increased spending on foreign-sourced highly paid professional services will put downward pressure on the dollar. Sending enough dollars overseas to pay for foreign doctors, lawyers, and economists may push the dollar down to the point that our manufacturing goods become more competitive on world markets. This would create millions of new manufacturing jobs.

The right plots long-term strategies along these lines. Progressives must think along the same lines to have a hope of winning.

The fundamental structure of economic debates has been turned on its head to favor the right. Progressives cannot hope to win a political debate if we think that we have an interest in inflating stock and housing prices. Given everything that is stacked against the progressive side in economic debates, we must at least know which way is up. Hopefully this book has helped to point the way.

References

AMA-OMSS Governing Council. 2007. "Report B: Medical Travel Outside the U.S."
American Medical Association: Report from the 2007 Annual AMA-OMSS Assembly Meeting.

Baker, Dean. 2002a. "The Housing Affordability Index: A Case of Economic Malpractice."
Washington, DC: Center for Economic and Policy Research.
http://www.cepr.net/documents/publications/housing_2002_12.pdf

Baker, Dean. 2002b. "The Run-up in Home Prices: Is It Real or Is It Another Bubble?"
Washington, DC: Center for Economic and Policy Research.
http://www.cepr.net/documents/publications/housing_2002_08.pdf

Baker, Dean. 2003. "The Artistic Freedom Voucher: An Internet Age Alternative to
Copyrights." Washington, DC: Center for Economic and Policy Research.
http://www.cepr.net/documents/publications/ip_2003_11.pdf

Baker, Dean. 2004. "Financing Drug Research: What Are the Issues?" Washington, DC:
Center for Economic and Policy Research.
http://www.cepr.net/documents/publications/intellectual_property_2004_09.pdf

Baker, Dean. 2009a. "The Housing Crash Recession and the Case for a Third Stimulus."
Washington, DC: Center for Economic and Policy Research.
http://www.cepr.net/documents/publications/intellectual_property_2004_09.pdf

Baker, Dean. 2009b. "Job Sharing: Tax Credits to Prevent Layoffs and Stimulate
Employment." Washington, DC: Center for Economic and Policy Research.
http://www.cepr.net/documents/publications/job-sharing-tax-credit-2009-10.pdf

Baker, Dean. 2011. "Work Sharing: The Quick Route Back to Full Employment."
Washington, DC: The Center for Economic and Policy Research.
http://www.cepr.net/documents/publications/work-sharing-2011-06.pdf

Baker, Dean and Rivka Deutsch. 2009. "The State and Local Drag on the Stimulus."
Washington, DC: Center for Economic and Policy Research.
http://www.cepr.net/documents/publications/stimulus-2009-05.pdf

Baker, Dean and Travis McArthur. 2009. "The Value of the 'Too Big to Fail' Big Bank
Subsidy." Washington, DC: Center for Economic and Policy Research.
http://www.cepr.net/documents/publications/too-big-to-fail-2009-09.pdf

Baker, Dean and Hye Jin Rho. 2009. "Free Trade in Health Care: The Gains from Globalized Medicare and Medicaid." Washington, DC: Center for Economic and Policy Research. http://www.cepr.net/documents/publications/free-trade-hc-2009-09.pdf

Baker, Dean and David Rosnick. 2011. "A Voluntary Default Savings Plan: An Effective Supplement to Social Security." Washington, DC: Center for Economic and Policy Research. http://www.cepr.net/documents/publications/cepr-savings-plan-2011-02.pdf

Baker, Dean, Robert Pollin, Travis McArthur, and Matt Sherman. 2009. "The Potential Revenue from Financial Transactions Taxes." Washington, DC: Center for Economic and Policy Research. http://www.cepr.net/documents/publications/ftt-revenue-2009-12.pdf

Bernanke, Ben. 1999. "Japanese Monetary Policy: A Case of Self-Induced Paralysis?" New Jersey: Princeton University. http://www.princeton.edu/~pkrugman/bernanke_paralysis.pdf

Bernanke, Ben. 2007. "Testimony of Chairman Ben S. Bernanke: The Economic Outlook," before the Joint Economic Committee, U.S. Congress, March 28. http://www.federalreserve.gov/newsevents/testimony/bernanke20070328a.htm

Bernstein, Jared and Dean Baker. 2004. *The Benefits of Full Employment.* Washington, DC: Economic Policy Institute.

Bishop, Paul C., Shonda D. Hightower, and Harika Bickicioglu. 2005. "Profile of Homebuyers." Chicago, IL: National Association of Realtors. http://www.realtor.org/Research.nsf/files/2005HBSonlineHighlights.pdf/$FILE/2005HBSonlineHighlights.pdf

Blinder, Alan and Mark Zandi. 2010. "How the Great Recession Was Brought to an End." West Chester, PA: Moody's Analytics. http://www.economy.com/mark-zandi/documents/End-of-Great-Recession.pdf

Bureau of the Census. 1980. "Statistical Abstract of the United States, 1980." Washington, DC: U.S. Department of Commerce. http://www2.census.gov/prod2/statcomp/documents/1980-01.pdf

Business Software Alliance. 2011. "Eighth Annual BSA Global Software 2010 Piracy Study." Washington, DC: Business Software Alliance. http://portal.bsa.org/globalpiracy2010/downloads/press/pr_global.pdf

Carroll, Christopher D. and Xia Zhou. 2010. "Measuring Wealth Effects Using U.S. State Data." Paper presented at the Federal Reserve Bank of San Francisco Conference on Empirical Macroeconomics Using Geographical Data on March 18, 2011. http://www.frbsf.org/economics/conferences/1103/Zhou.pdf

Center for Medicare & Medicaid Services (CMMS). 2011a. "National Health Expenditure Projections 2010-2020." Washington, DC: CMMS.
http://www.cms.gov/NationalHealthExpendData/downloads/proj2010.pdf

Center for Medicare & Medicaid Services (CMMS). 2011b. "National Health Expenditure Amounts by Type of Expenditure and Source of Funds: Calendar Years 1965-2020." Washington, DC: CMMS.
http://www.cms.gov/NationalHealthExpendData/downloads/nhe65-20.zip

Congressional Budget Office (CBO). 2011a. "Budget and Economic Outlook, Fiscal Years 2011-2020." Washington, DC: CBO. http://www.cbo.gov/doc.cfm?index=12039

Congressional Budget Office (CBO). 2011b. "Estimated Impact of the American Recovery and Reinvestment Act on Employment and Economic Output from January 2011 Through March 2011." Washington, DC: CBO. http://www.cbo.gov/doc.cfm?index=12185&type=1

Congressional Research Service (CRS). 2007. "U.S. Health Care Spending: Comparison With Other OECD Countries." Washington, DC: CRS.
http://assets.opencrs.com/rpts/RL34175_20070917.pdf

Crimmann, Andreas, Frank Wießner, and Lutz Bellmann. 2010. "The German Work-sharing Scheme: An Instrument for the Crisis." Geneva: International Labour Organization.
http://www.ilo.org/wcmsp5/groups/public/--ed_protect/---protrav/---travail/documents/publication/wcms_145335.pdf

Dunkelberg, William C. and Holly Wade. 2011. "NFIB Small Business Economic Trends." Nashville, TN: National Federation of Independent Business.
http://www.nfib.com/Portals/0/PDF/sbet/sbet201108.pdf

European Foundation for the Improvement of Living and Working Conditions (EFILWC). 2010. "Extending Flexicurity: The Potential of Short-Time Work Schemes." Dublin: EFILWC.

Feyrer, James, and Bruce Sacerdote. 2011. "Did the Stimulus Stimulate? Real Time Estimates of the Effects of the American Readjustment and Recovery Act." Cambridge, MA: National Bureau of Economic Research.

Freeman, Eric. 2003. "Barriers to Foreign Professionals Working in the United States." Washington, DC: Center for Economic and Policy Research.
http://www.cepr.net/documents/publications/professional_supplement.htm

Gagnon, Joseph, and Gary Hufbauer. 2011. "Taxing China's Assets: How to Increase U.S. Employment Without Launching a Trade War." *Foreign Affairs,* April 25.
http://www.foreignaffairs.com/articles/67810/joseph-gagnon-and-gary-hufbauer/taxing-chinas-assets

Greenspan, Alan. 2002. "Monetary Policy and Economic Outlook." Testimony before the Joint Economic Committee, U.S. Congress, April 17. http://www.federalreserve.gov/boarddocs/testimony/2002/20020417/default.htm

Harris, Brian. 2006. "Federal Home Loan Mortgage Corporation, Analysis." Moody's Investors Service, Inc. http://www.freddiemac.com/investors/pdffiles/fm2006_moodys.pdf

Hudson, Michael W. 2010. *The Monster: How a Gang of Predatory Lenders and Wall Street Bankers Fleeced America and Spawned a Global Crisis.* New York: Times Books.

International Monetary Fund (IMF). 2010. "A Fair and Substantial Contribution by the Financial Sector." Report to the G-20 Toronto Summit, Toronto, Canada, June 26-27. http://www.imf.org/external/np/g20/pdf/062710b.pdf

Iwry, J. Mark, and David C. John. 2009. "Pursuing Retirement Security Through Automatic IRAs." Washington, DC: Brookings Institution. http://www.brookings.edu/papers/2009/07_automatic_ira_iwry.aspx

Kirchhoff, Sue and Barbara Hagenbaugh. 2004. "Greenspan says ARMs might be better deal." *USA Today*, February 24. http://www.usatoday.com/money/economy/fed/2004-02-23-greenspan-debt_x.htm

Klein, Alec and Zachary A. Goldfarb. 2008. "The Bubble." *Washington Post*, June 15. http://www.washingtonpost.com/wp-dyn/content/article/2008/06/14/AR2008061401479.html

Krugman, Paul. 2009. "Failure to Rise." *New York Times,* February 12. http://www.nytimes.com/2009/02/13/opinion/13krugman.html

Lewin, Tamar. 2011. "Education Department Increases Its Regulation of For-Profit Colleges." *New York Times*, June 2. http://www.nytimes.com/2011/06/02/education/02gainful.html

Messenger, Jon C. 2009. "Work Sharing: A Strategy to Preserve Jobs During the Global Jobs Crisis." Geneva: International Labour Organization. http://www.ilo.org/wcmsp5/groups/public/---ed_protect/---protrav/---travail/documents/publication/wcms_120705.pdf

Milliot, Jim. 2010. "Book Sales Fell 1.8% in 2009, to $23.8 Billion, AAP Says." New York: Publishers Weekly. http://www.publishersweekly.com/pw/by-topic/industry-news/bookselling/article/42745-book-sales-fell-1-8-in-2009-to-23-8-billion-aap-says.html

Newzoo. 2011. "Total Consumer Spend 2010." Newzoo. http://www.newzoo.com/ENG/1575-Total_Consumer_Spend_2010.html

Organization for Economic Cooperation and Development (OECD). 2010. "Employment Outlook 2010: Moving Beyond the Job Crisis." Paris: OECD.

Organization for Economic Cooperation and Development (OECD). 2011. "Growing Income Inequality in OECD Countries: What Drives It and How Can Policy Tackle It?" Paris: OECD. http://www.oecd.org/dataoecd/32/20/47723414.pdf

Pear, Robert. 1997. "A.M.A. and Colleges Assert There Is a Surfeit of Doctors." *New York Times*. March 1.

Pew Research Center. 2010. "Americans Are of Two Minds on Trade." Washington, DC: Pew Research Center. http://pewresearch.org/pubs/1795/poll-free-trade-agreements-jobs-wages-economic-growth-china-japan-canada

Popper, National. 2010. "Andrew Cuomo, Steve Rattner Settle N.Y. Pension Fund Case." *Los Angeles Times*, December 30.

Ray, Rebecca and John Schmitt. 2007. "No-Vacation Nation." Washington, DC: Center for Economic and Policy Research. http://www.cepr.net/documents/publications/2007-05-no-vacation-nation.pdf

Ray, Rebecca, Janet C. Gornick, and John Schmitt. 2008. "Parental Leave Policies in 21 Countries: Assessing Generosity and Gender Equality." Washington, DC: Center for Economic and Policy Research. http://www.cepr.net/documents/publications/parental_2008_09.pdf

Reinhold, Rich. 2000. "Union Membership in 2000: Numbers Decline During Record Economic Expansion." *Illinois Labor Market Review*. Vol. 6, No. 4. http://lmi.ides.state.il.us/lmr/union.htm

Rosnick, David and Dean Baker. 2011a. "Representative Ryan's $30 Trillion Medicare Waste Tax." Washington, DC: Center for Economic and Policy Research. http://www.cepr.net/documents/publications/ryan-waste-2011-04.pdf

Rosnick, David and Dean Baker. 2011b. "When Numbers Don't Add Up: The Statistical Discrepancy in GDP Accounts." Washington, DC: Center for Economic and Policy Research. http://www.cepr.net/documents/publications/gdp-2011-08.pdf

Rosnick, David and Mark Weisbrot. 2006. "Are Shorter Work Hours Good for the Environment? A Comparison of U.S. & European Energy Consumption." Washington, DC: Center for Economic and Policy Research. http://www.cepr.net/documents/publications/energy_2006_12.pdf

Schmitt, John. 2008. "The Union Wage Advantage for Low-Wage Workers." Washington, DC: Center for Economic and Policy Research. http://www.cepr.net/documents/publications/quantile_2008_05.pdf

Schmitt, John. 2011. "Labor Market Policy in the Great Recession: Some Lessons from Denmark and Germany." Washington, DC: Center for Economic and Policy Research. http://www.cepr.net/documents/publications/labor-2011-05.pdf

Schmitt, John and Ben Zipperer. 2009. "Dropping the Ax: Illegal Firings During Union Election Campaigns, 1951-2007." Washington, DC: Center for Economic and Policy Research.   http://www.cepr.net/documents/publications/dropping-the-ax-update-2009-03.pdf

Shiller, Robert J. 2006. "Long-Term Perspectives on the Current Boom in Home Prices." *The Economists' Voice*, Vol. 3, No. 4.

Sun, Lena H. 1996. "Caught in the Middle." *Washington Post*, March 19.

Tax Policy Center. 2010. "T10-0188 - Department of the Treasury Revenue Estimates for Extension of 2001 and 2003 Tax Cuts and the Administration's High-Income Tax Proposals Impact on Tax Revenue (\$ billions), 2010-20." Washington, DC: Tax Policy Center. http://www.taxpolicycenter.org/numbers/displayatab.cfm?DocID=2785

United Nations Statistics Division. 2010. "Environmental Indicators: Greenhouse Gas Emissions." New York: United Nations. http://unstats.un.org/unsd/environment/air_co2_emissions.htm

U.S. Department of the Treasury and U.S. Department of Housing and Urban Development. 2011. "Reforming America's Housing Finance Market: A Report to Congress." Washington, DC: U.S. Department of the Treasury and U.S. Department of Housing and Urban Development.

Visser, Jelle. 2011. "ICTWSS: Database on Institutional Characteristics of Trade Unions, Wage Setting, State Intervention and Social Pacts in 34 countries between 1960 and 2010." Amsterdam: Amsterdam Institute for Advanced Labour Studies. http://www.uva-aias.net/208

Woo, Nicole. 2011. "Job Creation that Both Parties Can Agree On." Washington, DC: Center for Economic and Policy Research. http://www.cepr.net/index.php/blogs/cepr-blog/job-creation-that-both-parties-can-agree-on

Zandi, Mark and Cristian deRitis. 2011. "The Future of the Mortgage Finance System." New York: Moody's Analytics. http://www.economy.com/mark-zandi/documents/Mortgage-Finance-Reform-020711.pdf

About the Author (and his dog)

Dean Baker is an economist and the co-director of the Center for Economic and Policy Research (www.cepr.net). He is the author of *Taking Economics Seriously, False Profits: Recovering from the Bubble Economy, Plunder and Blunder: The Rise and Fall of the Bubble Economy, The United States Since 1980, The Conservative Nanny State: How the Wealthy Use the Government to Stay Rich and Get Richer, Social Security: The Phony Crisis* (with Mark Weisbrot), and *The Benefits of Full Employment* (with Jared Bernstein). He was the editor of *Getting Prices Right: The Debate Over the Consumer Price Index*, which was a winner of a Choice Book Award as one of the outstanding academic books of the year. He appears frequently on TV and radio programs, including CNN, CBS News, PBS NewsHour, and National Public Radio. His blog, "Beat the Press," features commentary on economic reporting. He received his B.A. from Swarthmore College and his Ph.D. in economics from the University of Michigan.

Biscuit is a 10-year old lapdog. He is retired from his career as unwanted pet. Biscuit's former owner surrendered him to the Washington Humane Society due to economic hardship. He went to foster care and was adopted quickly. However, his new owner returned him half a year later because of health problems. Biscuit quickly settled into his old foster home and this time was determined to stay. He succeeded. His foster parents adopted him after failing to find a home for him. Biscuit graduated from the Washington Humane Society's Learning and Behavioral Center with a degree in Well-Mannered Dog. He is currently in training for his Canine Good Citizen certificate and would love to become a therapy dog working in retirement homes. He lives in Washington, DC with Dean Baker, Helene, and his two sisters Kiwi-the-shep-mix and Olive-the-Doberman.

CPSIA information can be obtained at www.ICGtesting.com
Printed in the USA
BVOW030222160812

298035BV00001B/39/P